The Forgotten Forest

Published by the Witkin Gallery
415 West Broadway
New York, New York 10012

Library of Congress
Catalog Card Number 92-82860
ISBN 0-9118-9214-1

Printed in the United States

Book design by Eric Thoelke

The Forgotten Forest

Photographs by
Michael Eastman

Foreword by
William H. Gass

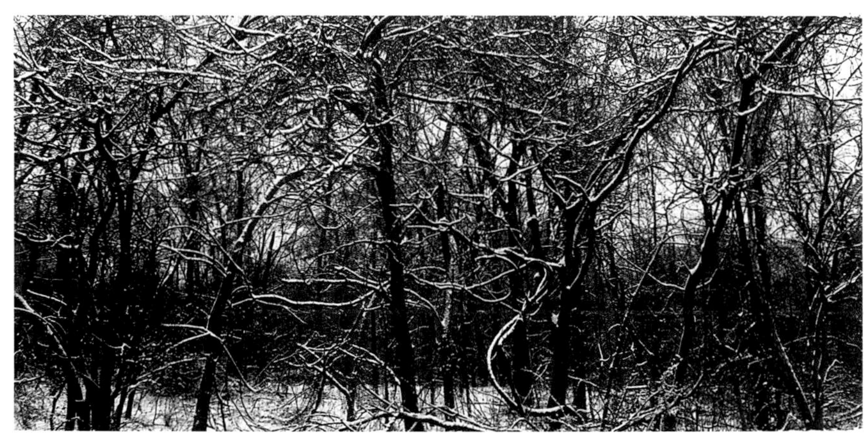

This book is dedicated to the memory of Pete Steefel

During this project there were several moments of awareness of being in the same place I had visited more than twenty years before, but looking at the same things with different eyes. These photographs are about discovering, rediscovering and the sheer joy of seeing. I found in this exploration a deep sense of renewal.

~ Michael Eastman

Acknowledgements

Many people have helped make the object in your hands a reality. My wife, Gayle, believed in this project even before the first photograph was made. Her support was always steady, and this book would simply not exist without her. Bill Gass honors me with his words. I am very grateful for his participation. Anabeth Caukins' enthusiastic assistance was given freely. Her much needed optimism was never more that a phone call away. Mary McElwain's energy was exceeded only by her generosity. Her efforts were herculean. Jan Broderick believed from the onset in the merit of these images. Her support means a great deal to me. Evelyne Daitz of The Witkin Gallery has my gratitude for providing this book with a more public venue. Our association brings me much joy. Eric Thoelke contributed to this project a deep commitment to quality. His vision has clarity and integrity.

There are others whose support was invaluable. They have my deepest appreciation. Phil Delano and Mary Engelbreit. Leo A. Drey. Marion Eastman. Emerson Electric Company. Michael Hoare and Nancy Collins. Greg Hoffmann of Green, Hoffmann and Dankebring. Interior Space Incorporated. Ellen Irons. Richard Jensen of Boatmen's National Bank of St. Louis. Janet and Tom Keller. David Mesker and A.G. Edwards & Son. Phoenix Creative Services. John Weil. Richard Wolchock.

THE PHOTO, THE FOREST, AND THE PARK

We never see the forest. We see only trees, though we say we see the forest when we see its trees. We cannot see the park either. We see this stretch of grass, that green hill, this pond, that pavilion, roadway, ballfield, wall or flowering weed. We remember, we guess, we imagine the rest. And we say we have been "to the Park," when we've driven along one street, parked in one place, swung only on one swing. So what do we see when we say we see photographs of such conceptual things?

The occasion for the photograph is fleeting, and its subject is invariably just a piece of something else, which is true even when a portrait pretends its pictured head is the whole world. Around the object of the image, there is always more, more in every direction, into the earth, high in the sky, over the rainbow, beyond the beyond. Whereas, outside the image of the object, past the edges of the print, there is nothing whatever, not even the abyss.

When we first look at a photograph, we see, in effect, totalities, not the dark marks or the fading rays of which the forest is composed, but immediately the milk-pale sky, the tree-and-cloud containing water, the dim ripple of a duck's wake. Furthermore, fine photographs, like the set which make up this book, are seen as sufficiencies. Pieces of the world, they are nevertheless wholes on their own. Even presented as diptychs, or married pairs, they keep their own names, maintain their own forms. When our inventory of the photograph begins, however, we pick it to pieces, and as our scrutiny of details, from bark scar to intrusive shadow, continues, we shall naturally note this particular bridge, bush, or bit of broken stone, this stain, that hint of bloom beneath a pile of brush, a flick of light from something otherwise lost in shadow, but these nameable elements will now be parts of the photograph, not portions of the world. If we realize that the forest and the park are totalities of which we encounter only fragments, and if we understand that the camera snaps up similar bits only to offer its images as wholes, then we know that the role of the photographic subject as a part of a wider world must also be imagined, because photographs are not perceptions, and it is safer to say of these that they are photos taken *from* the park than to say they are pictures *of* the forest.

Nothing here tells us a cloud, a leaf, a patch of snow, is temporary. Nothing warns us that, in a moment, the light will slide off inside a mist, or that a pool's smooth complexion will be ravaged by rain.

The park, of course, is made of moments; *they* are its real trees; but the photograph comprises *a* moment, one very small one, one smaller than we experience, so that in addition to the space which, by implication, surrounds the subject of the image, there is all that time, that before and after, that on and on. These are slices of life indeed, then: these motionless microtomes of moving clouds and growing grass and dripping trees.

The photographer waits out the clock, stalks the right time, surveys the scene like a hungry lion looking for its prey, but it is the camera which leaps at an unsuspecting ray, and thus fixes the position of the sun; which seizes the motion of a leaf in its teeth, and makes off.

How beautiful the world is to the gray-eyed. For inside our common crayon-colored realm – vulgar, loud enticing, but concealing too – lies this other measure, these shades of the one great gray which runs between a pure and spotless white to a black like no one's night, and which is a vibrantly sensitive register of the range of visual reality: of what can be known, and therefore of what absorbs light, what reflects it, what permits its passage and what prevents it, what concentrates it like a polished lens, what scatters it like cast grain, dissolving a scene into spatter and dapple. We have no names for these grays, the grays the leaves wear under their public greens, the grays which plant stems and grass blades scratch on the sky, or that almost imperceptible line, in Michael Eastman's stunning photograph of the encounter of a soft dark branch with softer water, which lies across the image of these entering or emerging twigs like a crack across cream.

What is captured for us here is an abundant luminosity, a luminosity of space on the one hand – sky, water, meadow – and the luminosity of the dense land as well – bush deep, trunk thick, moss soft – light almost as a liquid, light living in all things, for even in shade it is not altogether gone, even among occluding clouds it is alive as their lightning, and this tranquil yet vigorous presence allows the oaks which reside and rise inside a pond's reflection – the poles, the boat bottom, the long empty dock, a bombastic sky – to possess an equal palpability, an equal presence of the shadow with its substance, and permits us to feel the forest floor is itself a mirror, and that we are looking, not at fronds and grasses, at thickets and tangles, but at roots, as indeed, we sometimes are, at thoughts transposed as treetops, at calculations, as though a beech dared to show us its toes or decay its destination.

A park is a population: of lagoons, creeks, bridges, buildings, walks, walls and fences, playing fields, roads and paths – we can count its benches, picnic tables, trash cans, grills; whereas a forest is a festival of weeds and leaves, patches of damp and of filtered light, drifted snow and pond ice, of elements and items beyond interest and any census. A forest is made of repetitions, a park of spaces; one is all about clearing and order, care and use, the other about collision, competition, natural wildness. Parks must be kept up; they are like gardens. Forests profit from human neglect and avoidance, and represent the best interests of the planet. Forests go about their business. Parks go about ours. A Forest Park is a contradiction.

In these photographs, which are such passionate precisions that even in a woodlot, where tree trunks normally erupt from the earth like cemetery stones, and details disappear into a darkness which stands for the limit of our normal sight, we can observe a distant line of trees, a small lost car, a patch of flower-covered ground, with a distinctness we find only in the near at hand. The blindness of the camera to anything but its single sensitivity allows it to create this illusion of clarity, an illusion which paradoxically adds to our information rather than subtracting from it, and contributes to that luminosity which is such an outstanding quality of Michael Eastman's photographs. Indeed, within these small and sharply focused squares, we can now see more than our own freely ranging but blurry surveys could hope to achieve.

This camera does not see what can be seen. It sees what's there. Yes, we think we see the forest when we see the trees, but, in fact, we do not even see trees; only someone blind might feel those names scarred in the bark, now almost wholly swollen over, the way the camera catches them, or appreciate the holes which arrowheads have driven in the frame and stuffing of their target. Alas, the reality of our eye is always appearance.

But if the photograph achieves a particularity in all its parts we cannot normally achieve, where is the bustle, the shout of children, the creak of swings, the whirr of wheels, the hiss of the wind? Here light stands still as held breath. The heart has stopped in front of death. See how the sky hangs as motionless in its own air as in the pane of a pond, and a tree leans both ways, under and over water, and a bench remains empty forever of any visitor. A wet path, a snowed tree, a little light at rest upon a leaf: they have become visual forms, fixed, unfunctional, final, above all, complete, because, unlike universals, they have no range, and unlike laws, they have no scope.

Now and then a person appears in this park, but each is a far off figure, a natural entity like all the others, no different than a sawed log. So a special sort of solitude is realized within these windows, these four by fours from a forest, a park, late and early in the day, through several seasons of the year, and during a significant period of the photographer's life. There is, of course, the stillness seen so easily in the snow that's been planted with a pitchdark tree, or in the tilt of a boat against a pier, or in the clear uninterrupted passage of a pole from its rise to its reflection, and there is the emptiness contained in many scenes, even in images of grasses, vines, and undergrowth, which fill the foreground like a fence; but particularly in pictured playing fields and benches, an altogether unoccupied chair, a knoll, a stone park building, alone as if all of the world had gone home; but not as if abandoned, not as if rejected, none of them lonely, rather as if satisfied by their own solitude, content with their own plain yet pure being, because in a forest, in a park, everything is surrounded while being a part of the surroundings, nothing is solitary, only alone; and subordination, hierarchy, importance, are values we bring to the view, whereas the camera cares equally about all: can we detect some slighting of shade or reflection, as if they were unreal? are the broken, the fallen, the marred, whatever's dying, scorned? are small things snubbed, humble things ignored?

God said, let there be light, in order that we might pursue photography, and discover the light which is the life in these things, as if it had risen to the surface of every object in a landscape like a blush, so that each skyline, so darkly indented, so deeply and irregularly cut, each cloud, shadowed by the coasting earth below it, seems made of its own breath, each of its external relations internal to it, as if every tree projected its neighbors, and, in its turn, reflected them. Atget's parks have a similarly generous integrity. And the tremble of the water as the light returns, the fragile delicacy of most shadows, are all which distinguish their inverted or negated forms from those that make claims to substance.

Here, in the park, earth, air, light, and water meet – the ancient elements – and in these photographs, appearances mingle with realities, and the stream of time is stopped; now there is nowhere for the world to hide, the fugitive has been caught.

If we play in the park, if we pick our way through the forest, passing through either like a loud wind or skittish squirrel, we nonetheless soon leave for other environments. Perhaps our trash fills a barrel or a footprint stays or we bear away a weed which, undisturbed, had interest; but in the photograph, the photographer's eye remains, with its aims, its values, its themes, and these are also what we see when we say we see the forest in the photo; for that presence is as essential as the grays which compose each image, as ubiquitous as the light by which all of them are made – we know that – yet how, precisely where, in what distant bridge or broken wall or streaming sky, are we to find him? not as a small figure, surely, sitting on a T-shaped dock, at the margin of some pond-shaped pond, or even in a ring of leafless larches, let alone some patch of damp grass shining as though its divinity had just been announced.

We find him in all these pictured things, we are inclined to say, but most of all in their arrangement: if not in the broken wall, then in the juxtaposition of that wall with an equally shattered sidewalk, with the breach of land by water, and the puncture of sky by trees, through the music of those grays, their values, and the positioning of compositional paths, the layering of eyelines, the recession of lights and darks, the repetition of details, the duplication of shadows and reflections, the use of a foregrounded bench, for instance, to measure a distant band of trees, and, above all, the play, as throughout the park they appear, of verges, margins, and edges, with one another, of points of meeting: of a branch with bright air, a stretch of muddy bank with the water which besogs it, roads with grass, thickets with clearings, as well as the placement, in the park and in the photographs, of the marks of human presence – wall, walk, statue, car – marks which multiply, which intensify our absence – an absence which, among these almost noumenal entities, dominates the overall effect they have on me.

Because, of course, another eye is here, too, sizing up what has already been thrice-sized, since the park is a Park and not a forest, and has consequently been designed, and then seen, and then photographed, and finally perceived through and with and within these images by you and I; and we, you and I, will follow our fancies – what is to prevent it? we shall respond to this or that square-sided scene in one way while to another in another; we shall page past one image, maybe the contour of the Planetarium, with a Philistine nod of recognition – that's what that is! I recognize the contour! – and linger elsewhere, smacking our lips at something picturesque – a ruined wall from the 1904 Fair, possibly; how we fancy our own eye, don't we? yet our eye is an idler, these photographs should tell us that; our eye will wander rather vainly in search of the familiar in this park of which many of us are so familiar; though it won't matter really, if we've ever set foot in it, not if we remember to surrender our conceit, to resee these – so fully – reseen things, and find the feeling in them, to discover how beautiful the world is when at a standstill, for one thing.

The Forest and the Park, the camera shot and its subject, this volume and the signless world, Michael Eastman on Monday or Michael Eastman at another time, then you here and you over there, moreover me: we are all so different, aren't we? and if "Forest Park" is a misnomer, these photographs are all, from the Park's point of view, misleading too; since nothing is wed to its shadow the way these benches, bushes, trees, and bridges are to theirs; no pond so permanently filled with the same image as these are with their reflections; no light lies like a liquid upon real slopes; moreover, no forms will be found on our next walk like those which organize these pages; yet all of us, as other as we each are, meet here, in this splendid collection, where a community of park and forest, sense and concept, object and image, feeling and seeing, normally at odds in most selves is – I think – wonderfully achieved, and in a way so direct, yet mysterious, we must point at it in order to explain.

I can cite the simple way three light poles, aiming at almost the same vanishing point, turn into the phallic spires of yucca plants; or the way the confrontation between park and forest is dramatized in the powerful upthrust of a tree trunk which first appears to part a path and then to throw its dark shape across a stone house like heavy cancellation, with a consequence which is nevertheless a harmonious balance between visual halves; or the way a wreath of leaves replicates the rings of a freshly sawed stump: a violent act of man rendered peaceable by these orbiting signs of the oak's demise.

I can mention the vibration in our attention between the park as a subject which holds our visitorial interest, and the photograph as an artist's careful composition which elicits our admiration; or that between the anonymity of all those objects in the landscape – little lakes and gentle slopes and banks and bushes, trees and traffic signs and wide wide skies – and their uniqueness in these remarkable prints, where the personality of a forked path or trunk's lean is unmistakable.

Possibly my favorite photograph is made of three tree trunks on a tough rough ground, one so similar to the other, they are constantly exchanging spacial places, vying like bullying boys to be kings of the image; yet branch and ground fold into a single lively and syncopated plane, their common texture acting as a common bond.

Finally, I can readily imagine how different our various responses to a dense thicket might be, to grass in a tangle like uncombed hair, to the death of a fallen log, the shatter of a struck tree, the swallow of a wall by the woods, and to all those images which are claustrophobically dense with vines, fronds, tendrils – creeping, scratchy, clutching things – or show growths which seem diseased; and yet I can also remain confident of the great solitude, the luminous peace, in these scenes, where things which are opposed by other elements in nature, or are distracted by the trivializing attention of picnickers, find in these photographs their natures truly depicted, fully extended, richly revealed.

It is the rarely realized aim of any art to satisfy innumerable demands, those both reasonable and outrageous; to harmonize every chord though played by differently jealous fingers; to bring into its peaceable kingdom the most beastly and poisonous creatures, even if they be as widely opposed and apart in their ways as forest and park, image and object, your eye, my eye, the skillful eye of its artisan, and, of course, as is amply demonstrated here, the omnivorous eye of the art.

William H. Gass
St. Louis, Missouri
August, 1992

The Plates

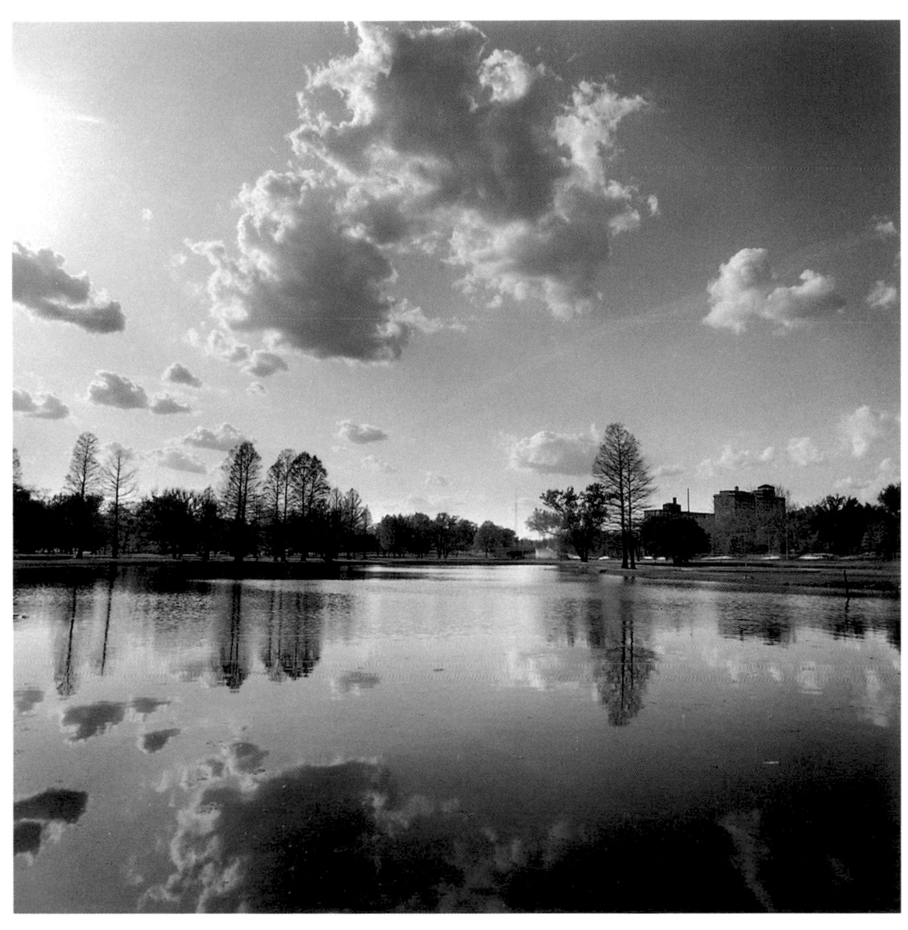

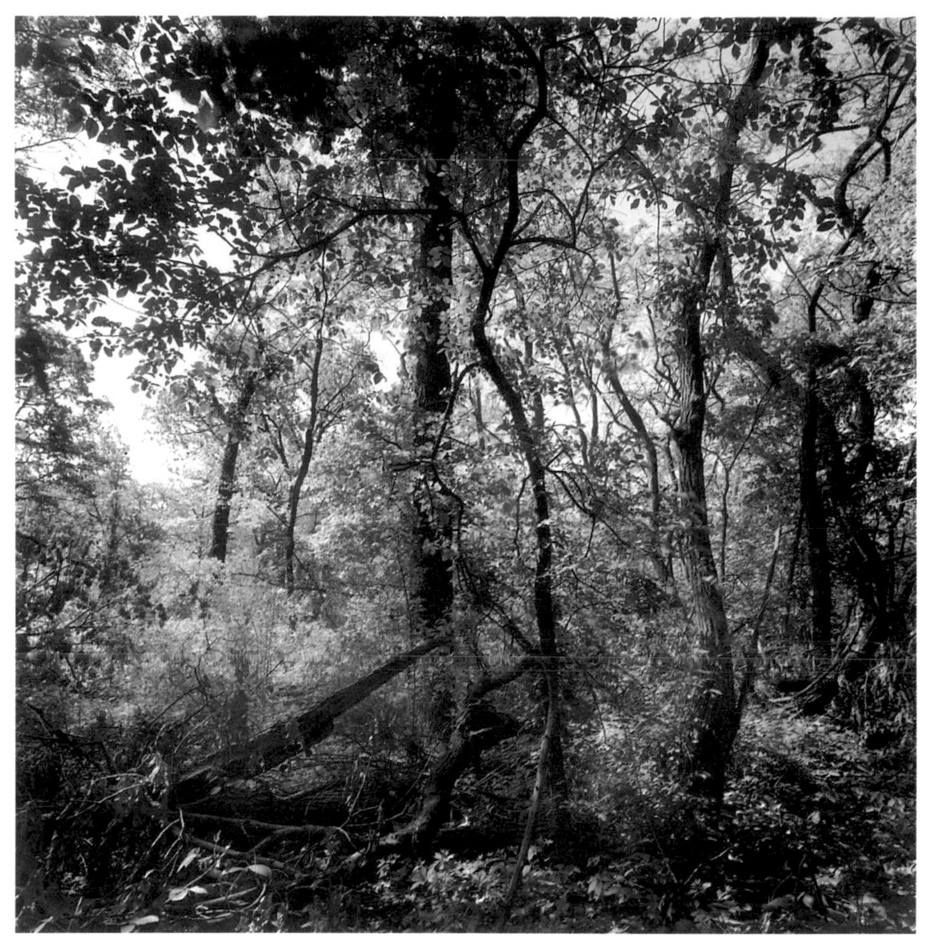

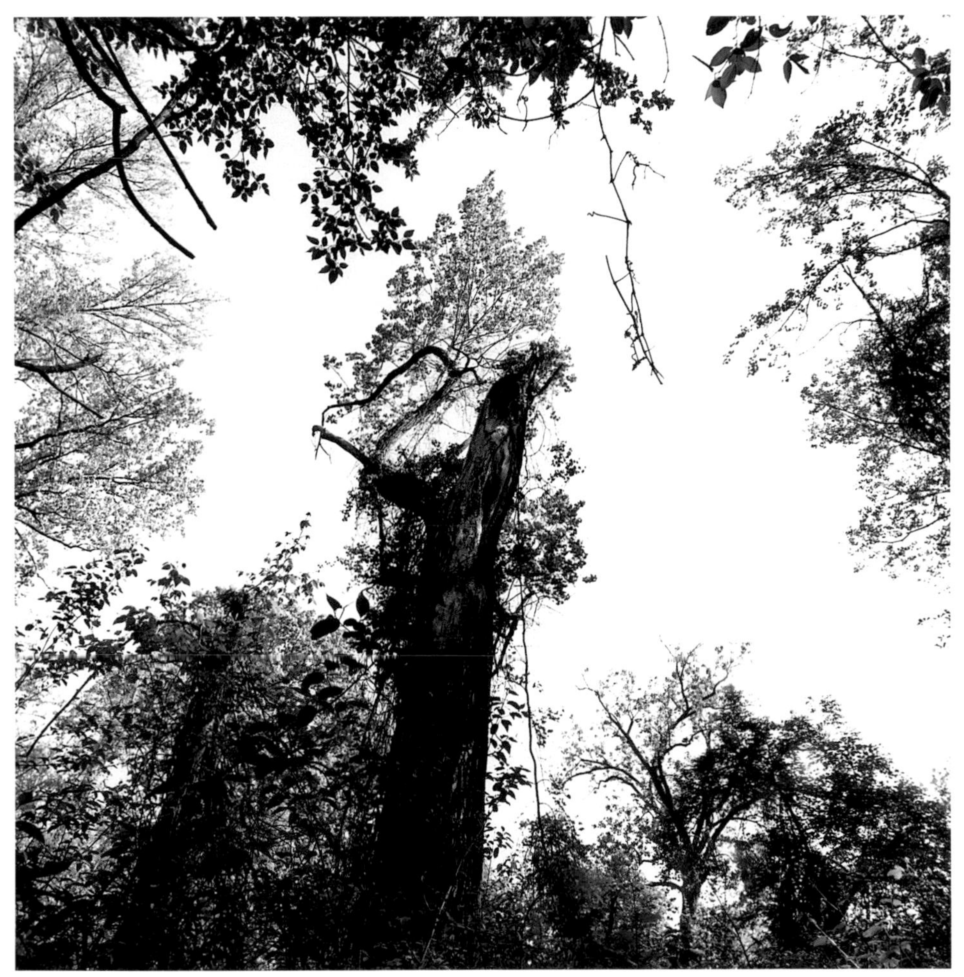

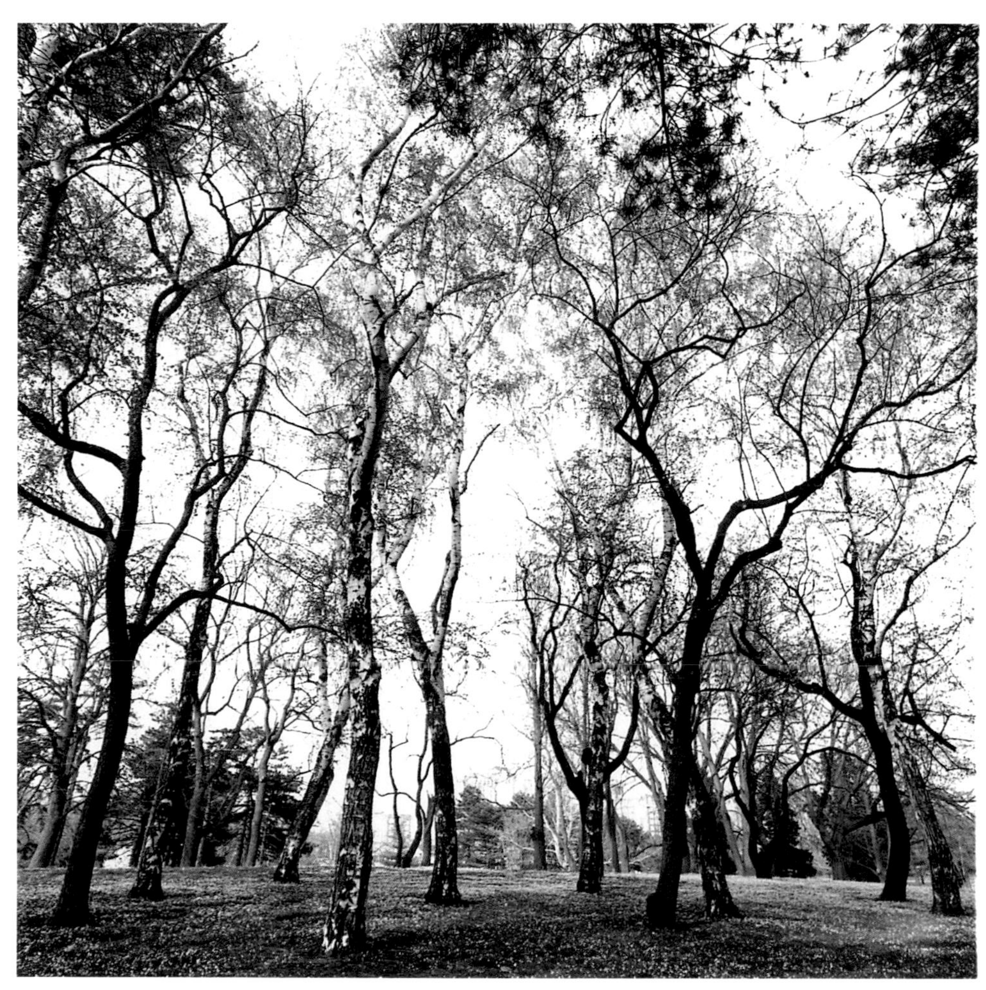

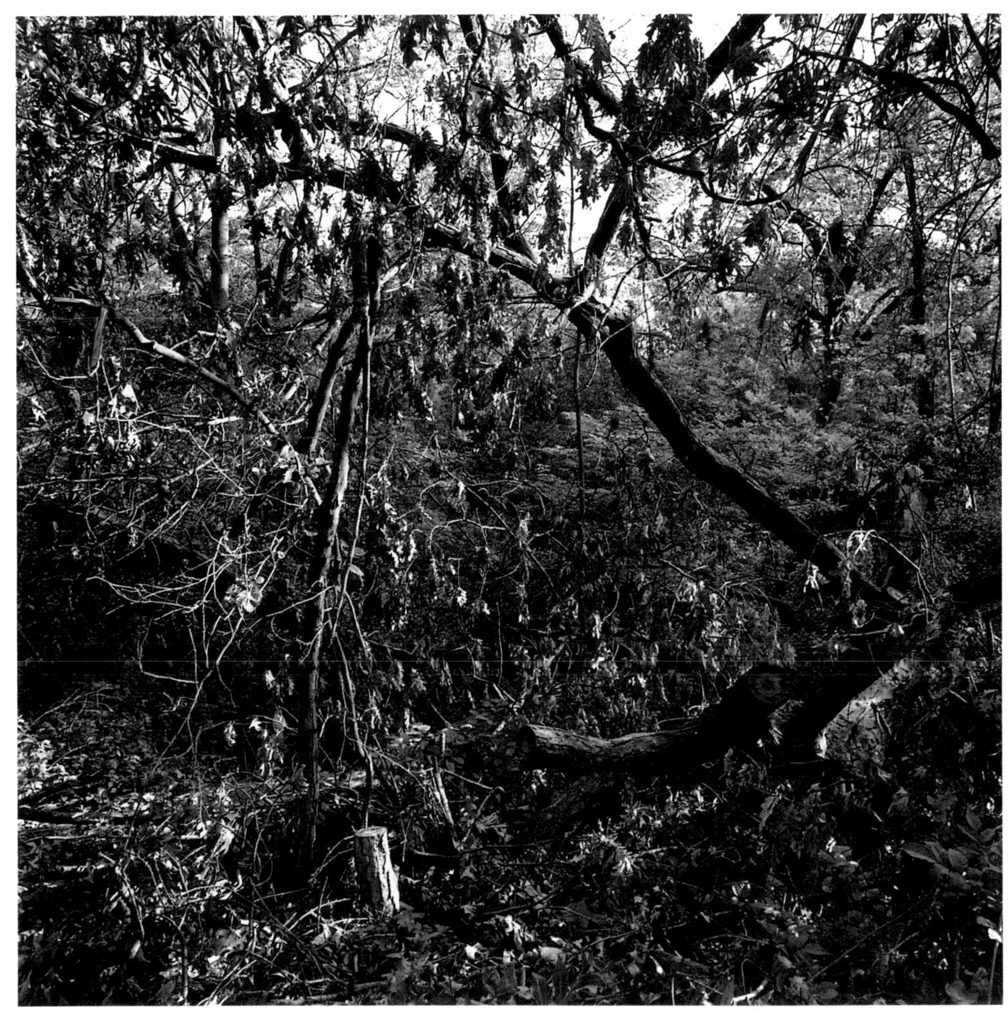

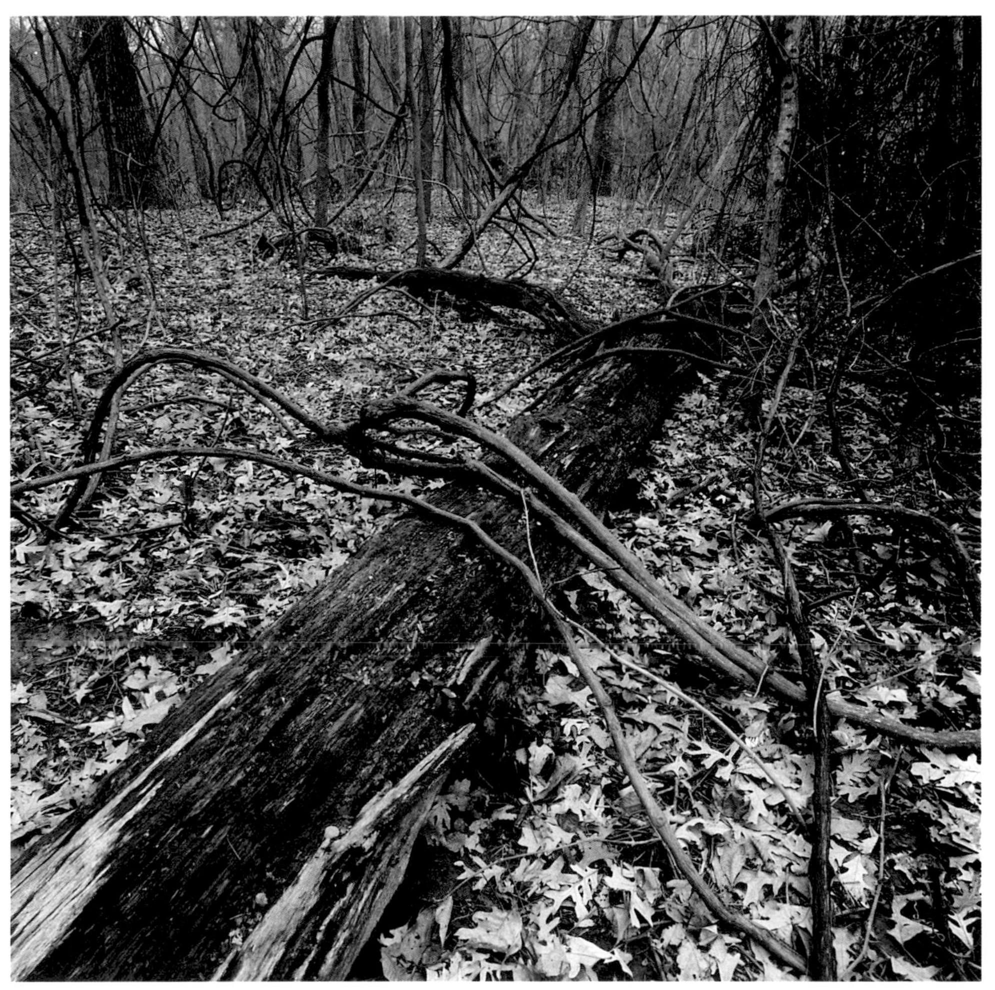

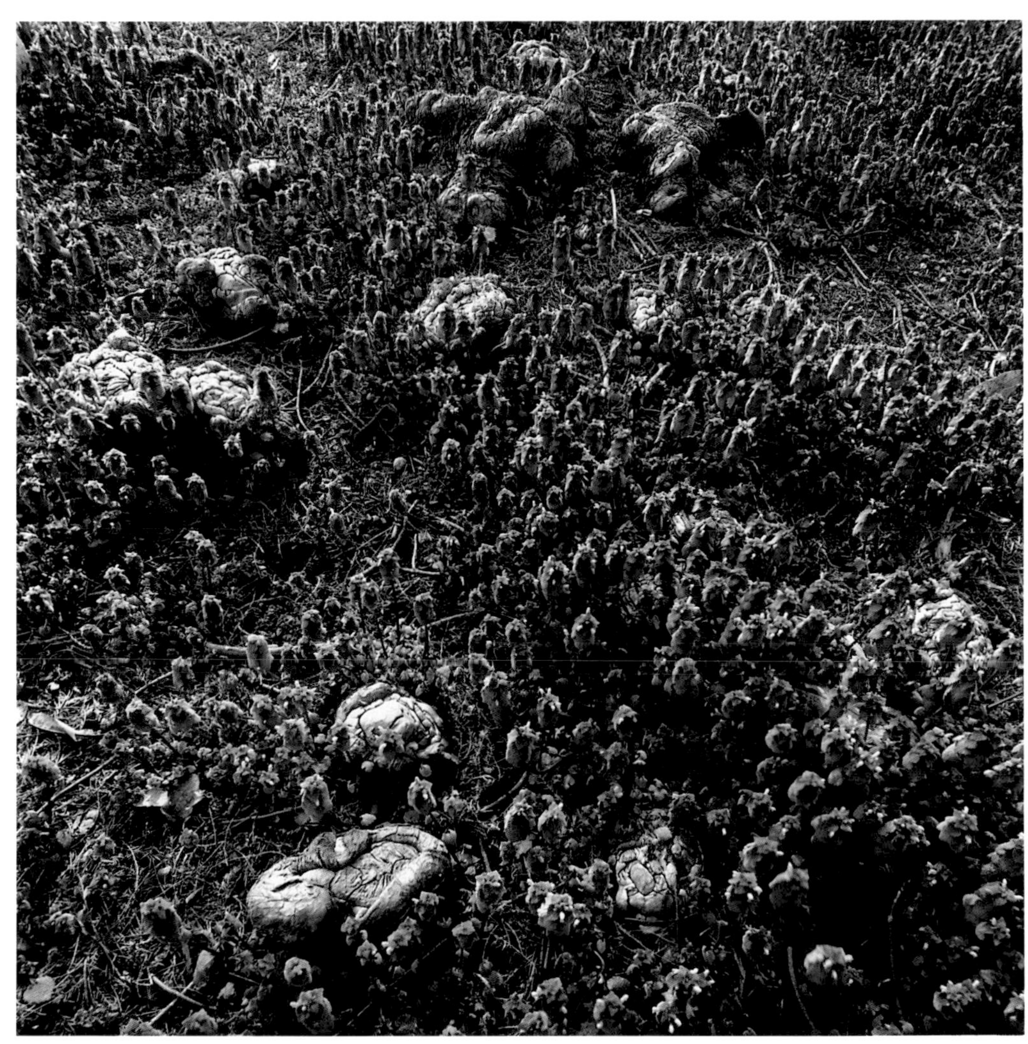

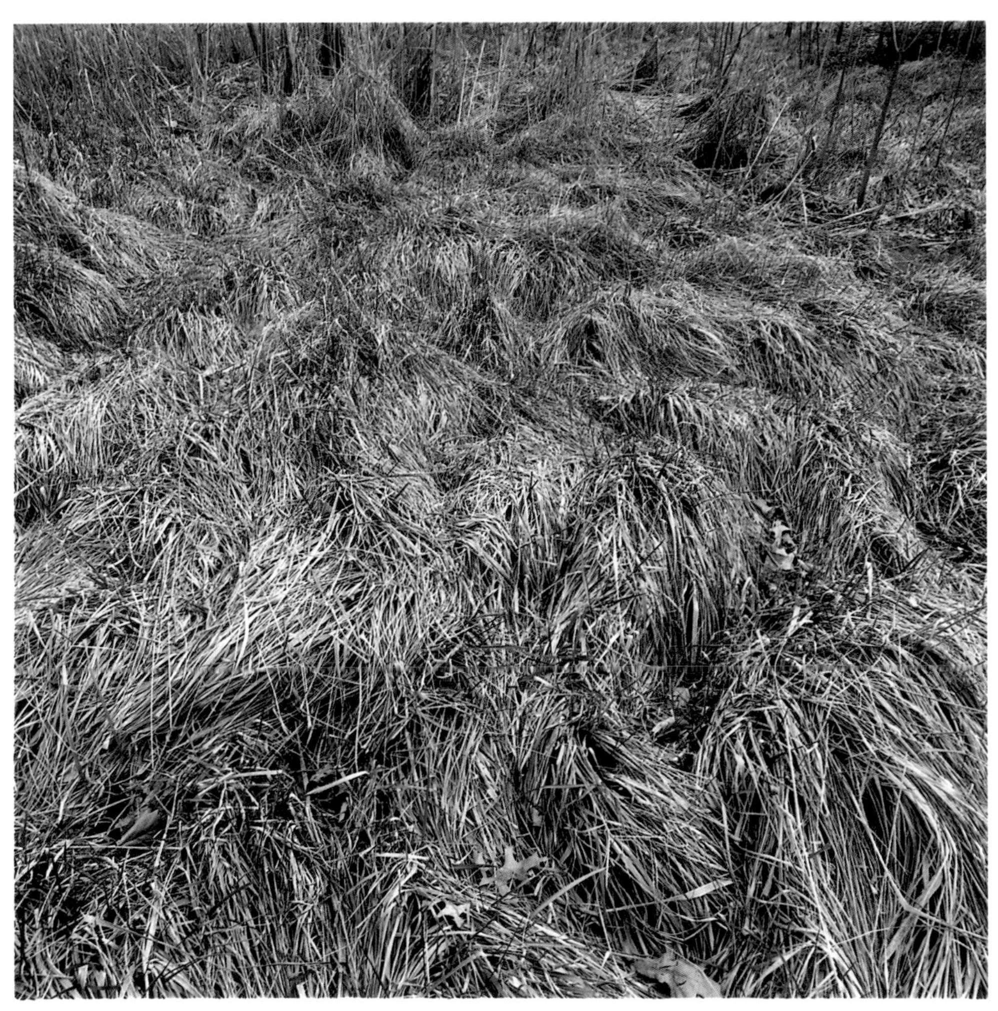

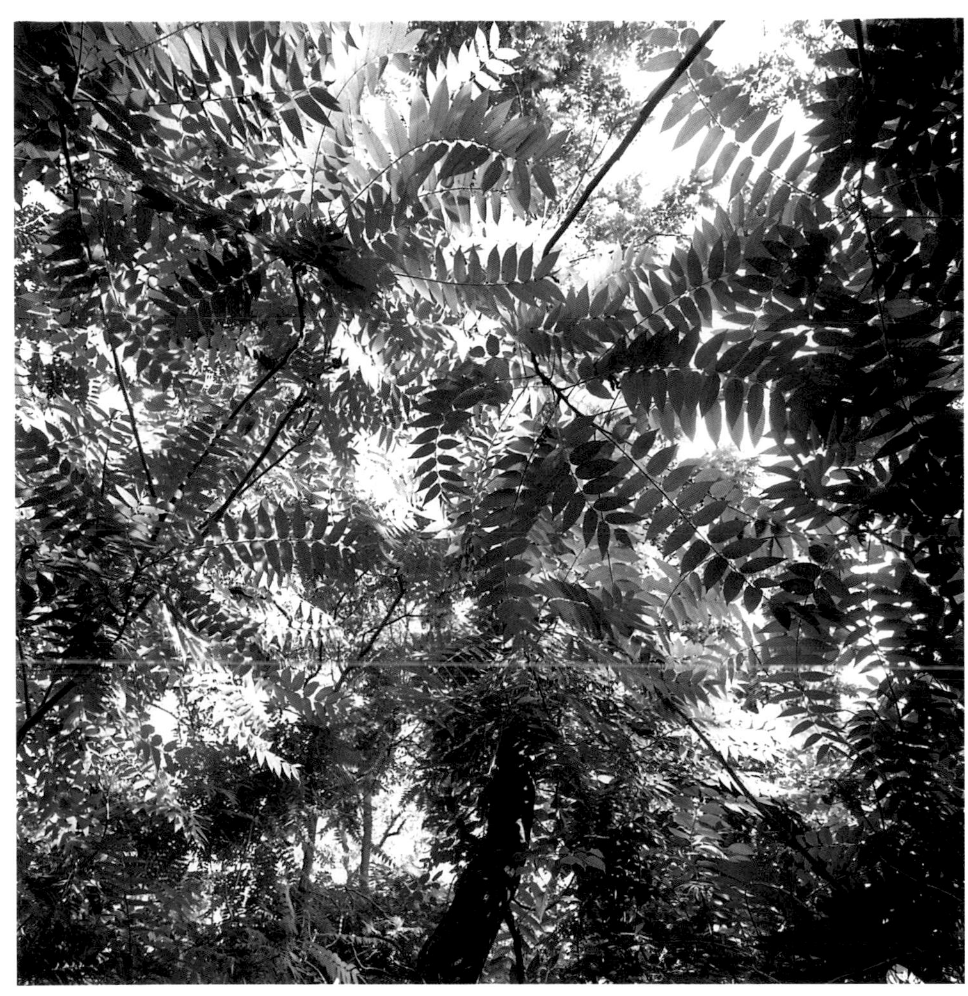

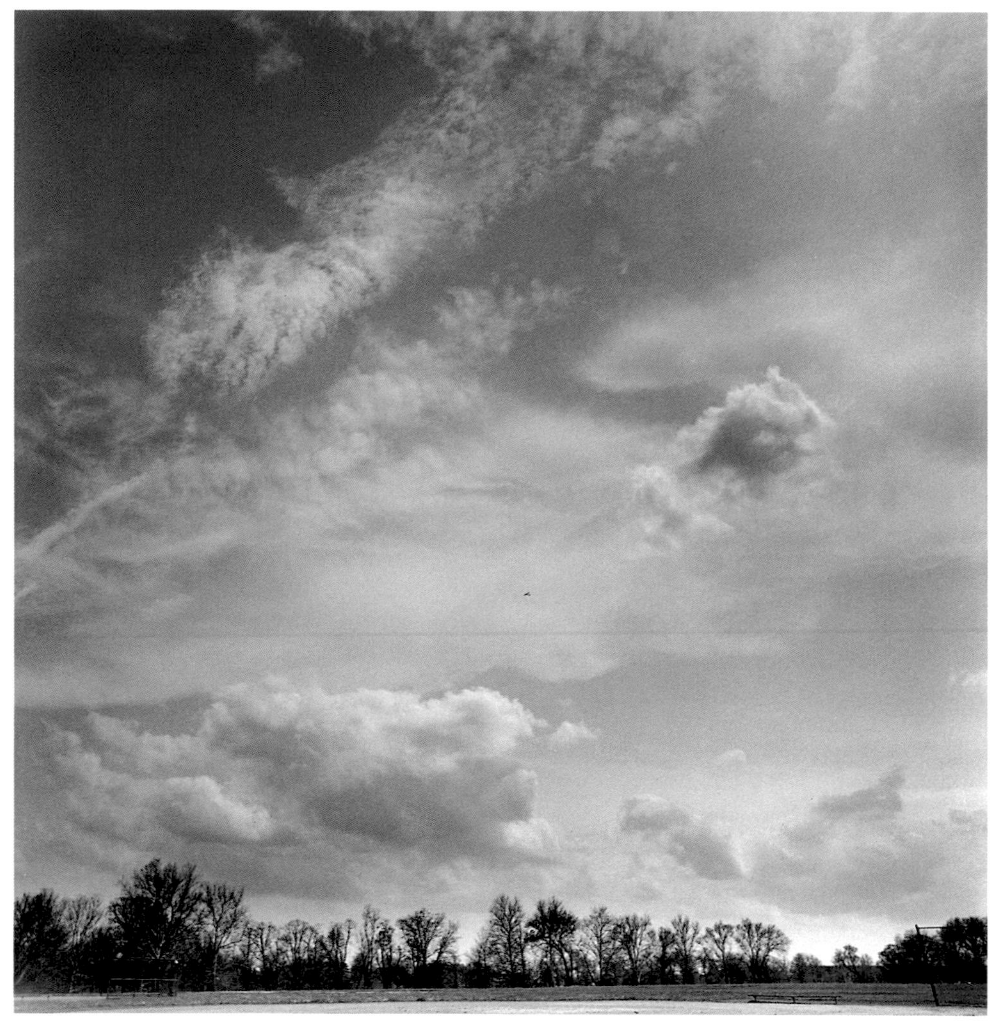

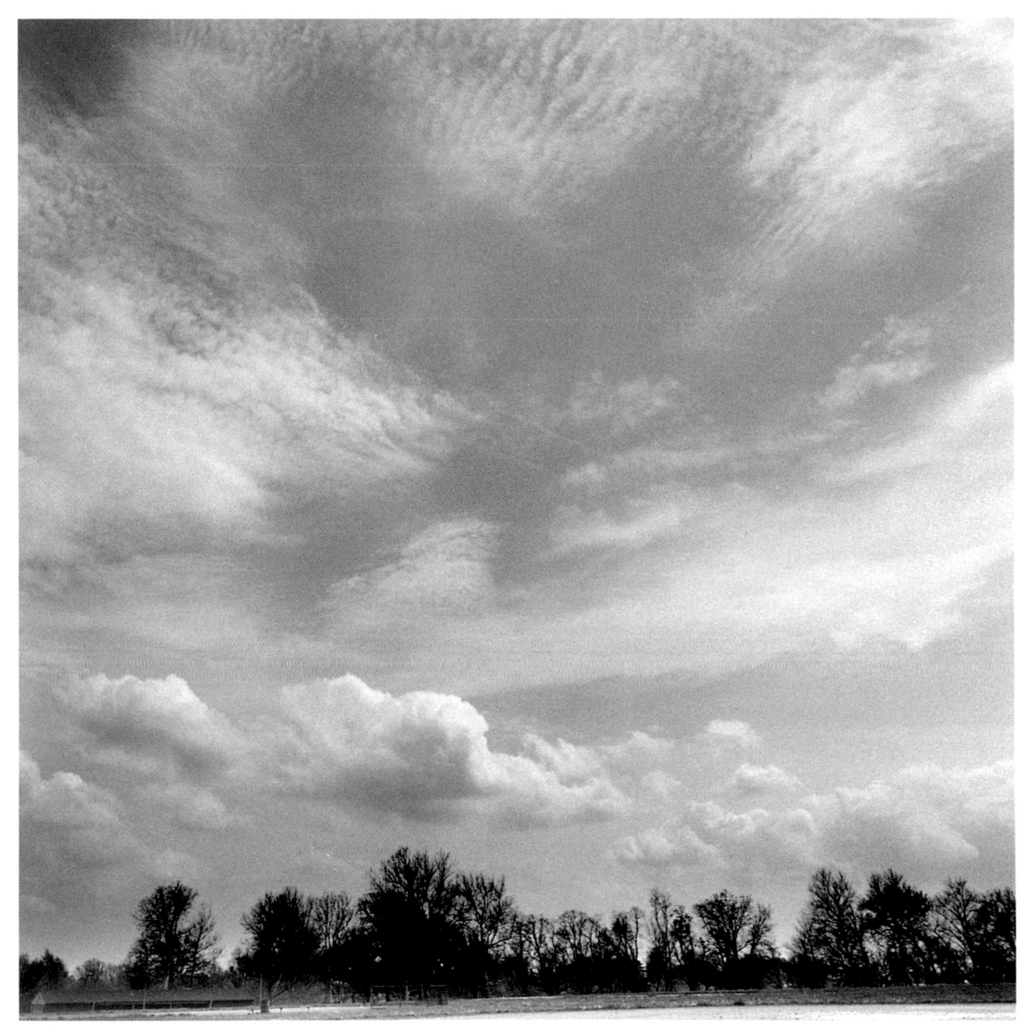

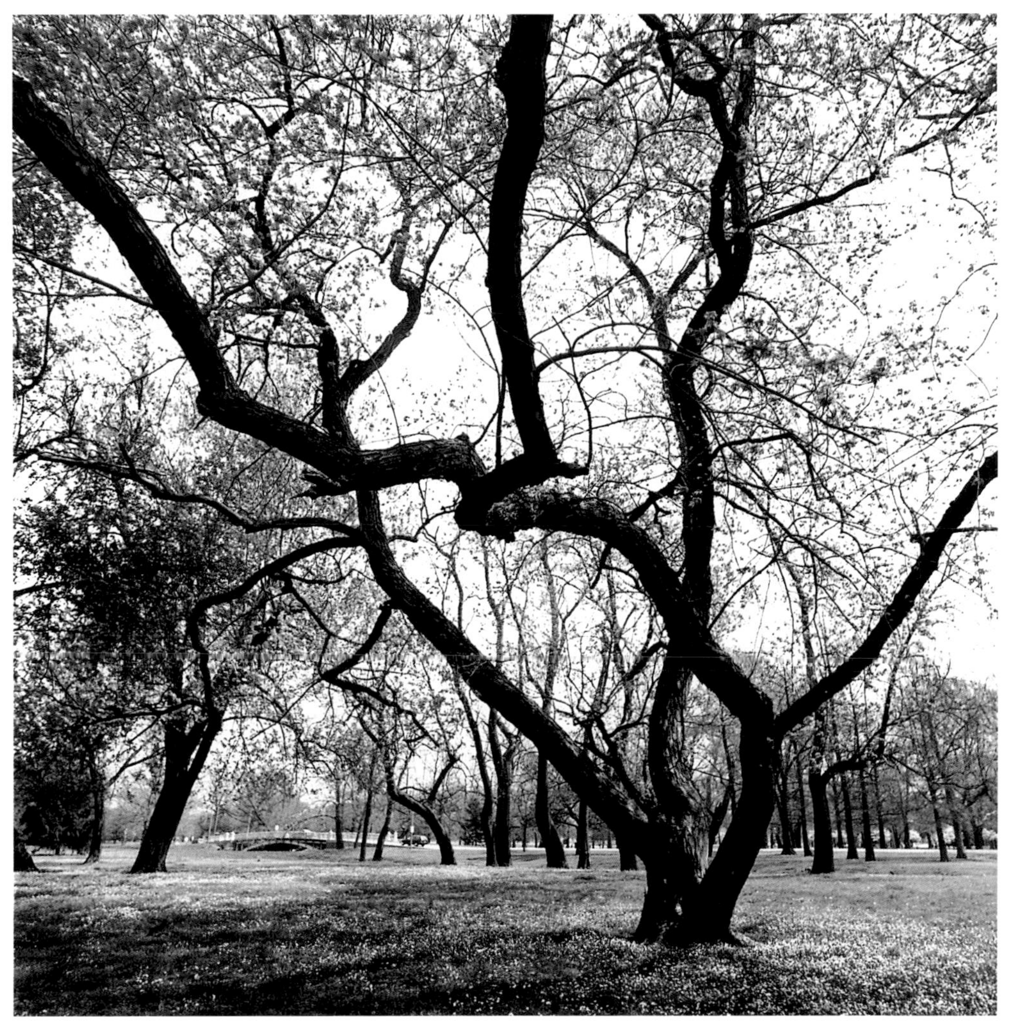

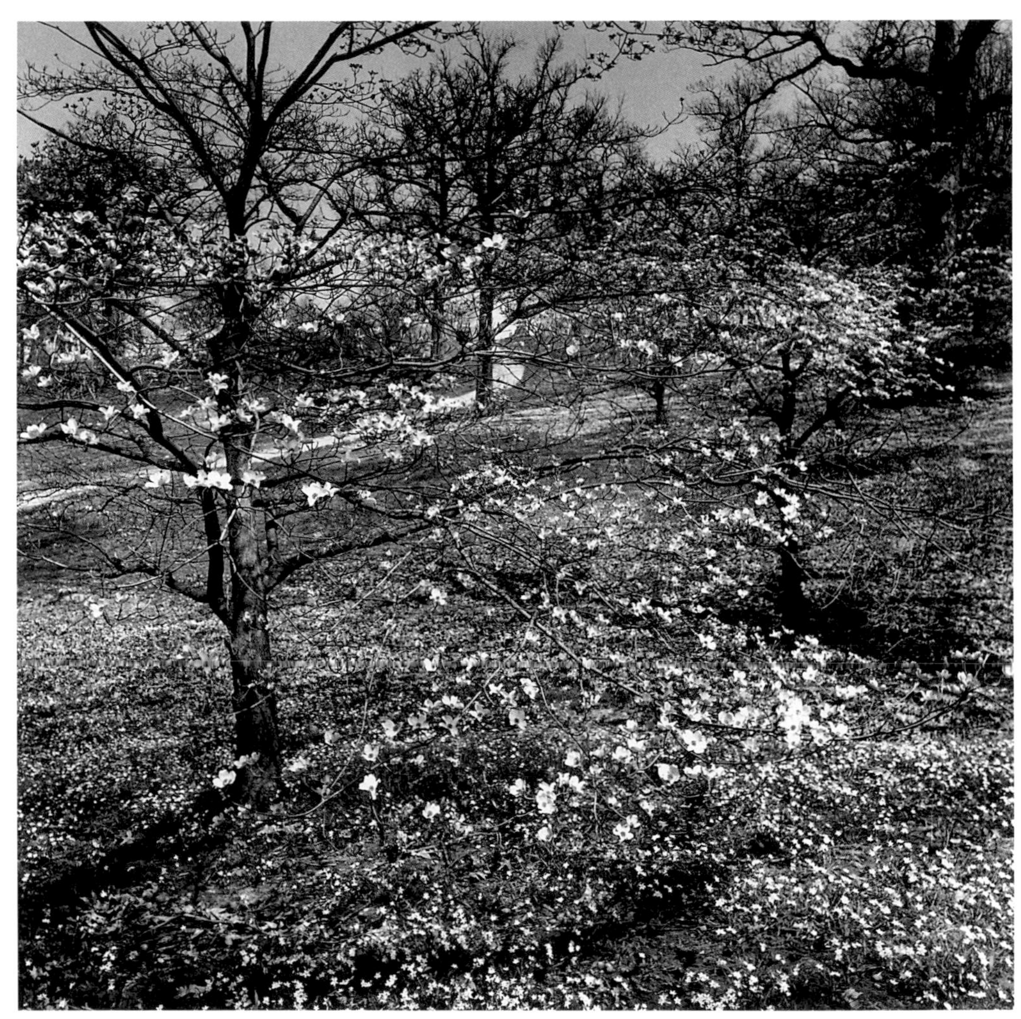

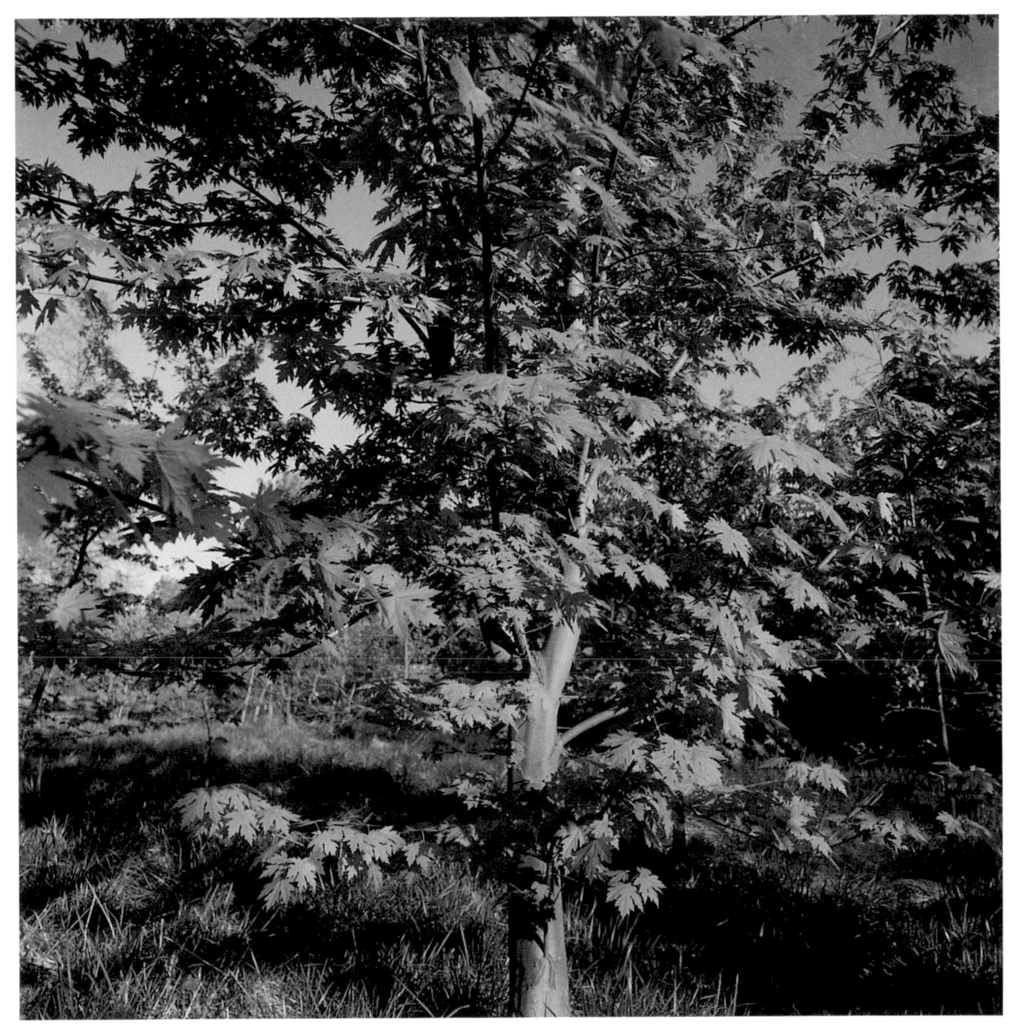

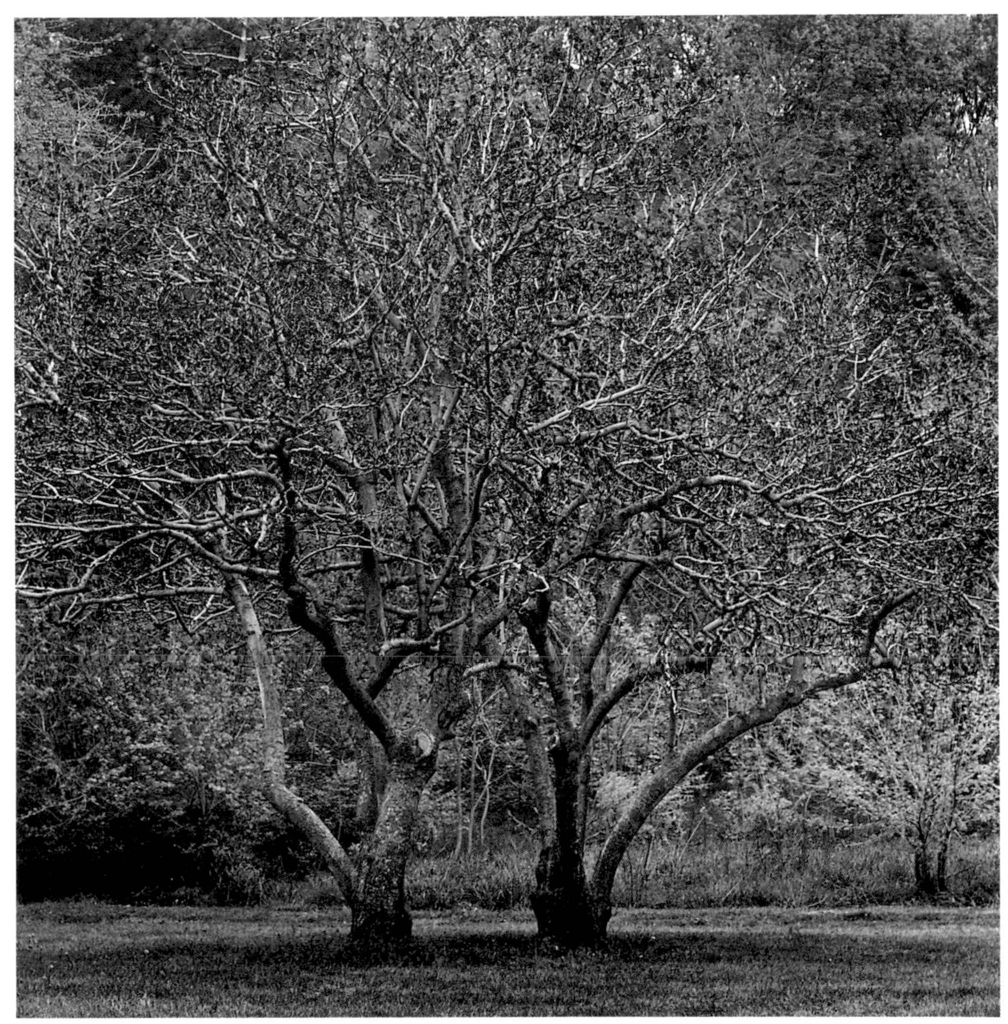

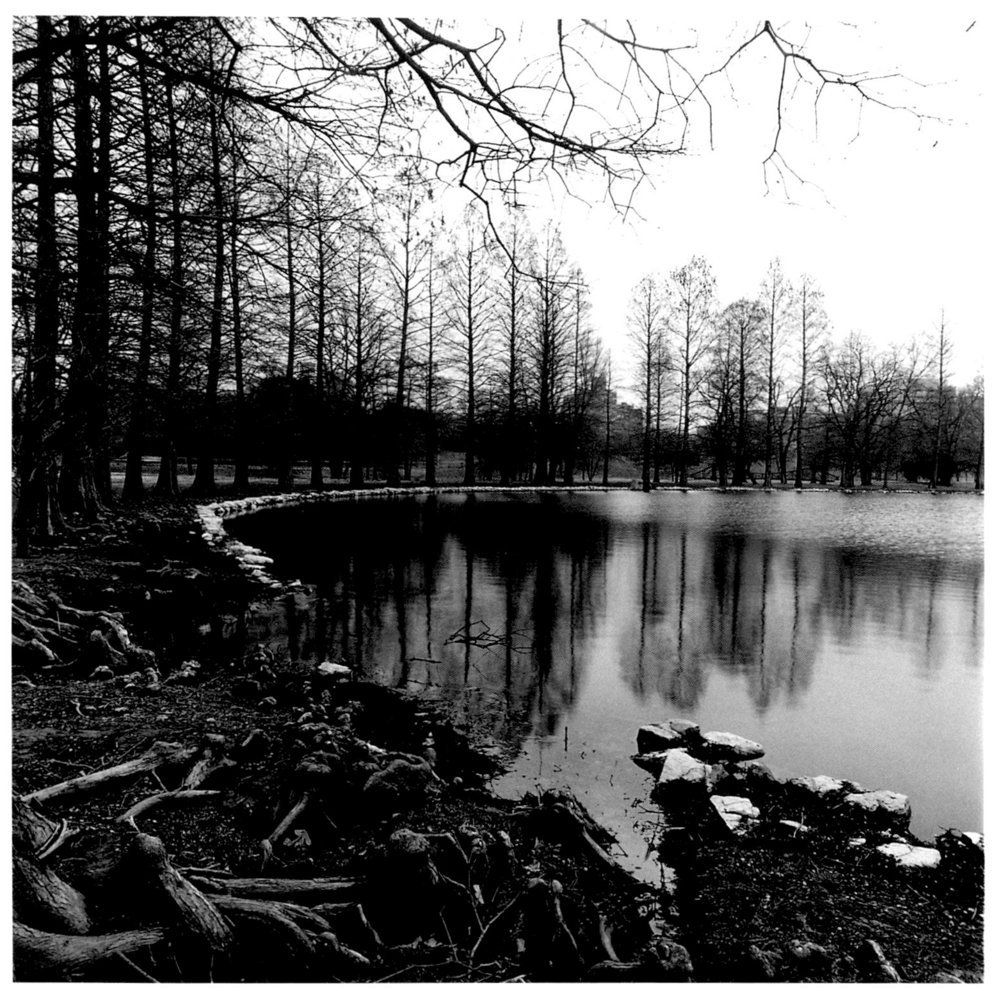

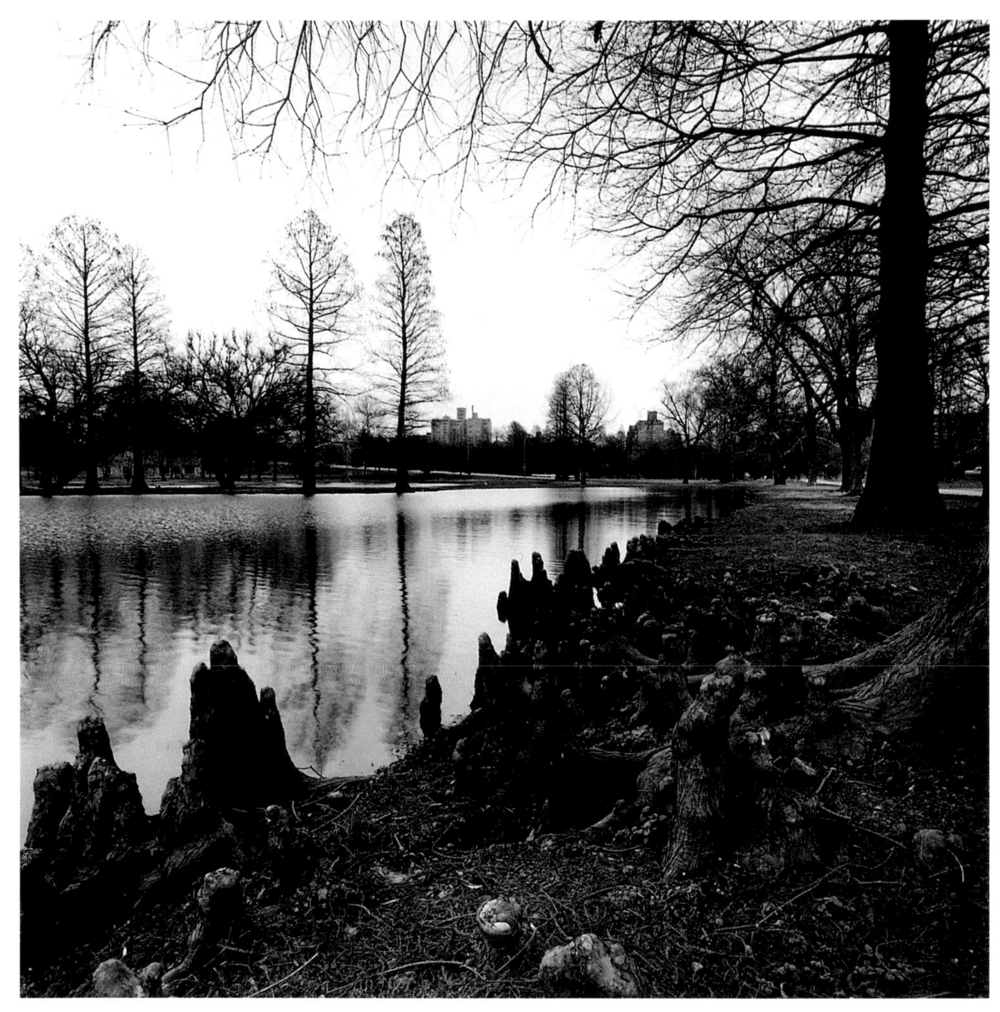

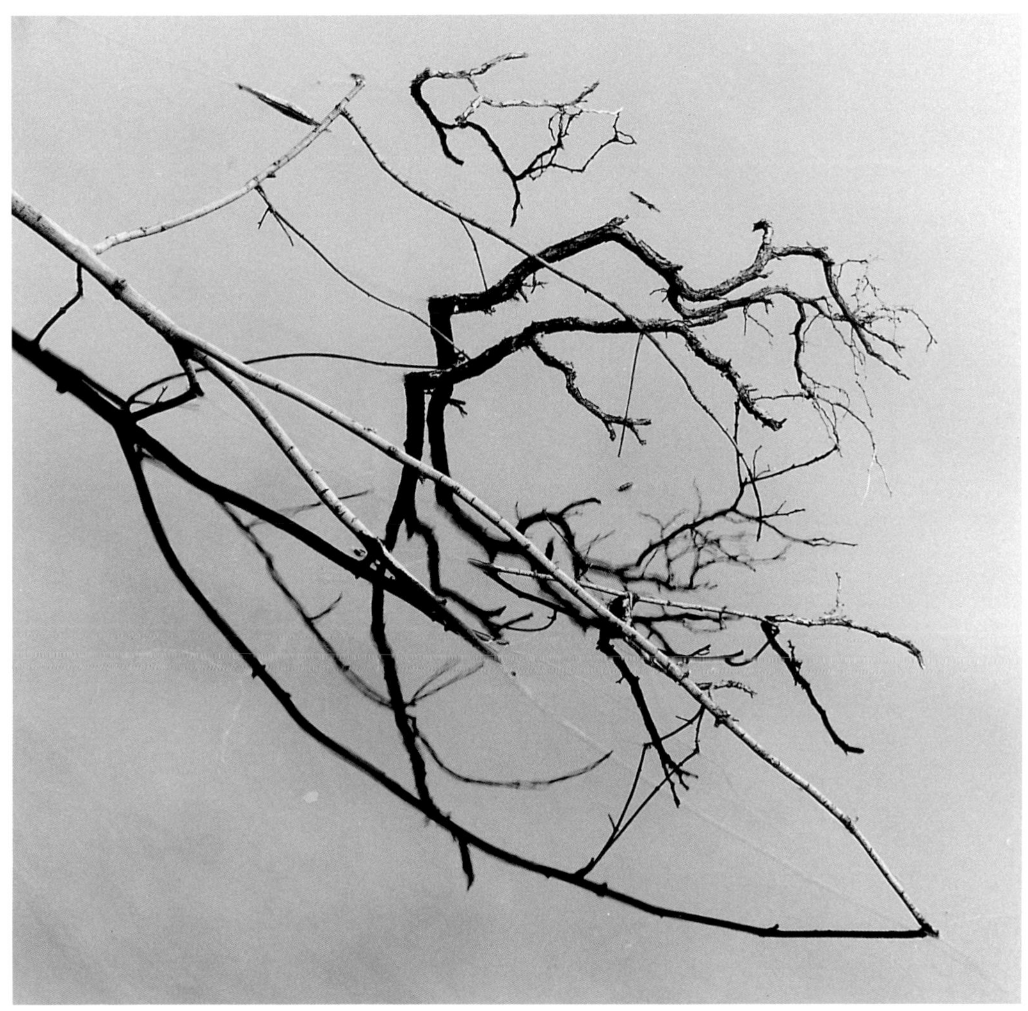

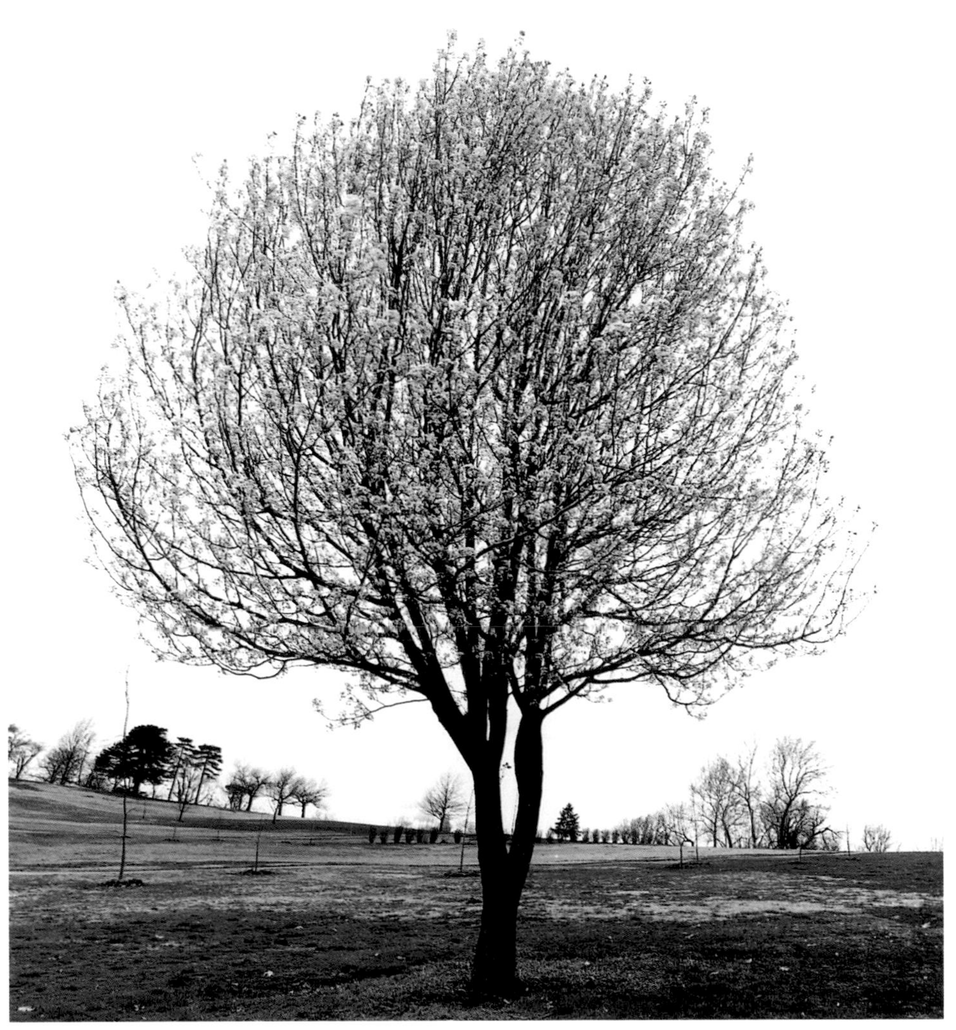

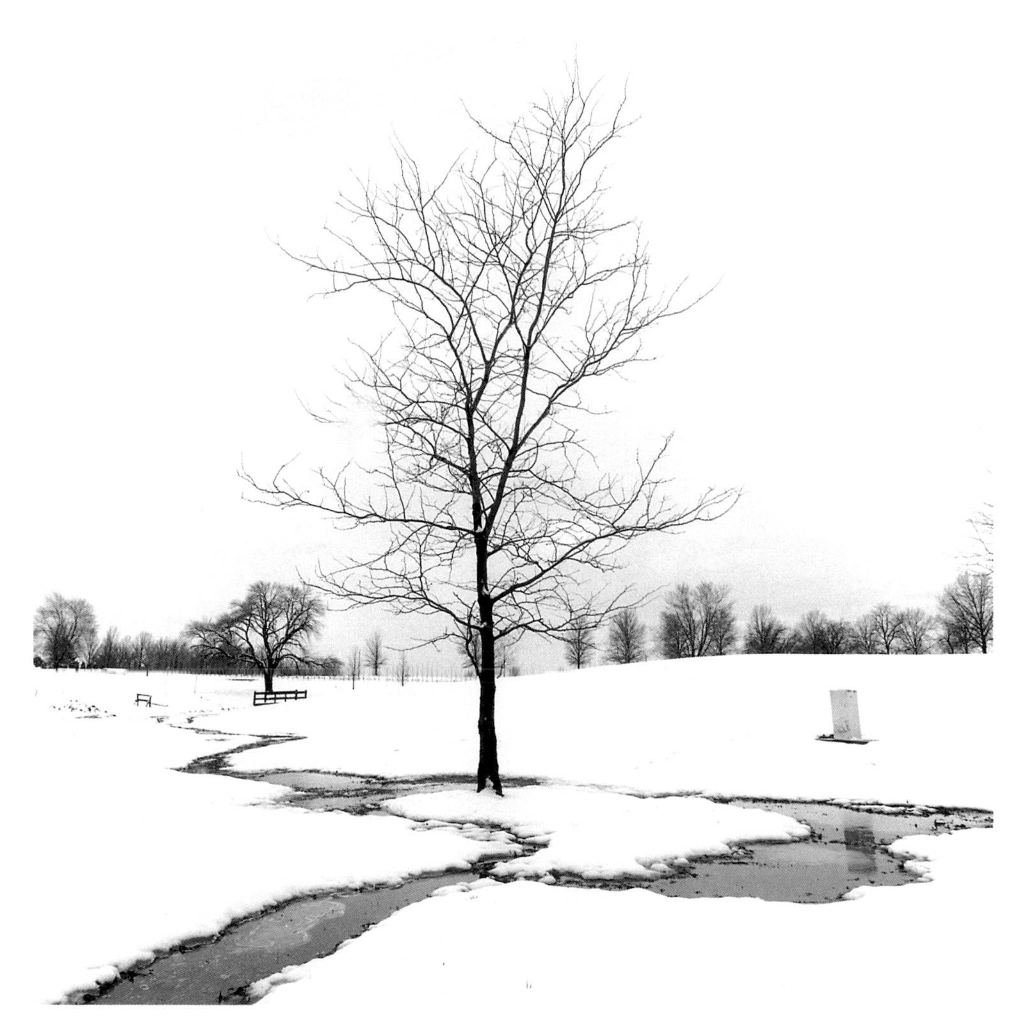

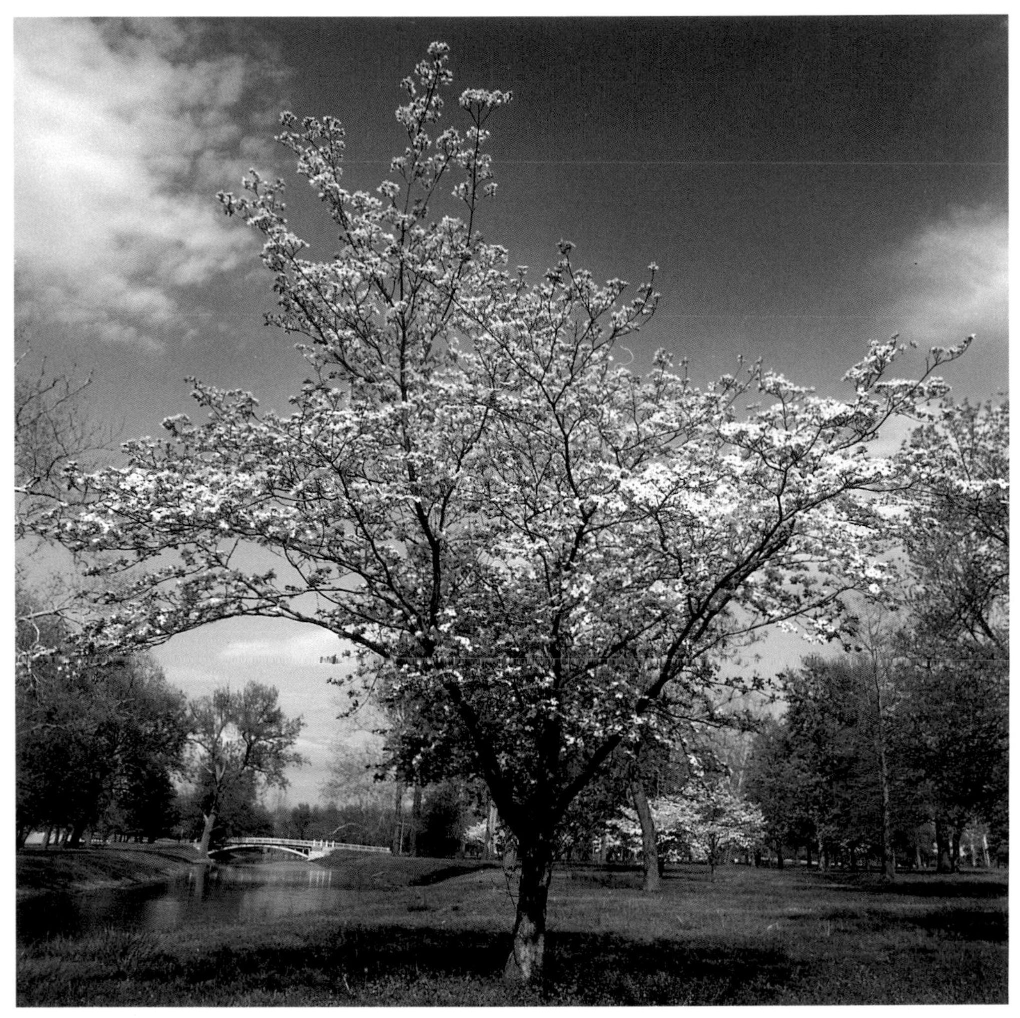

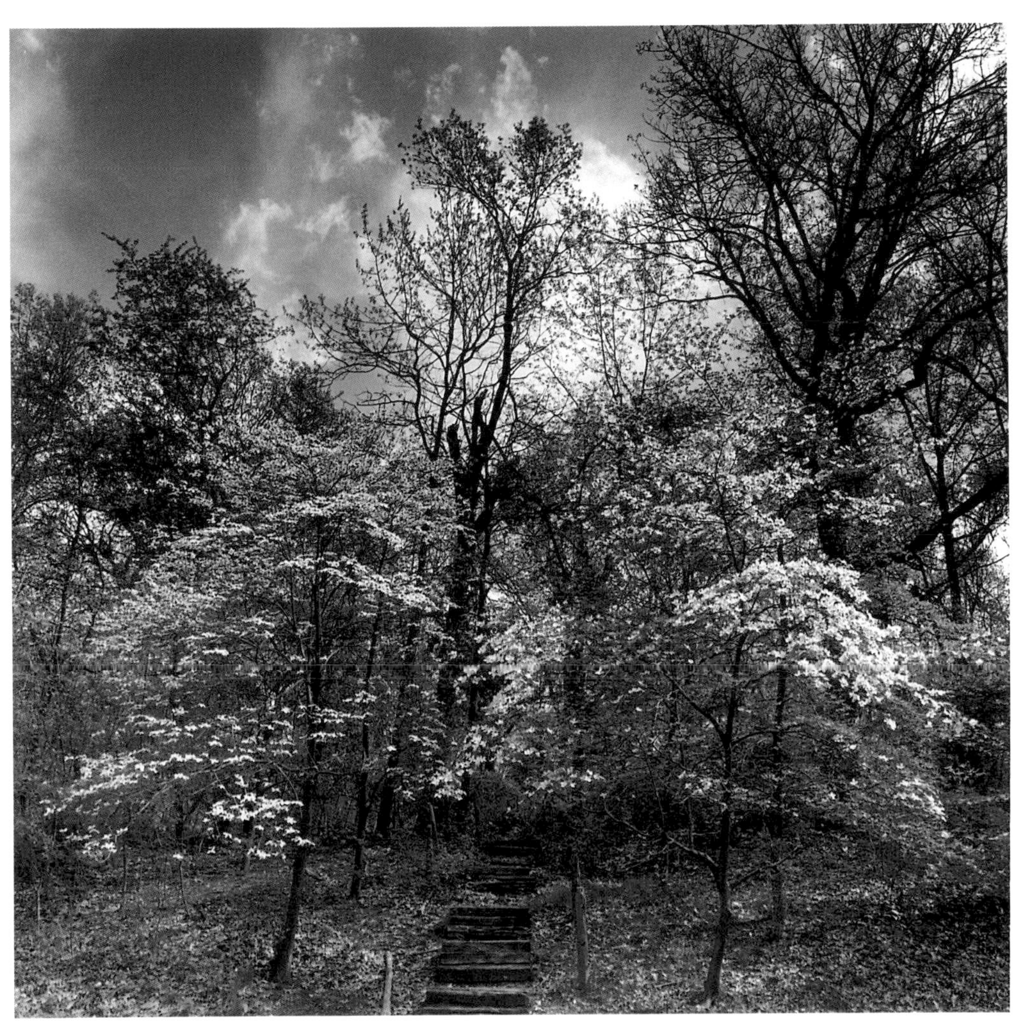

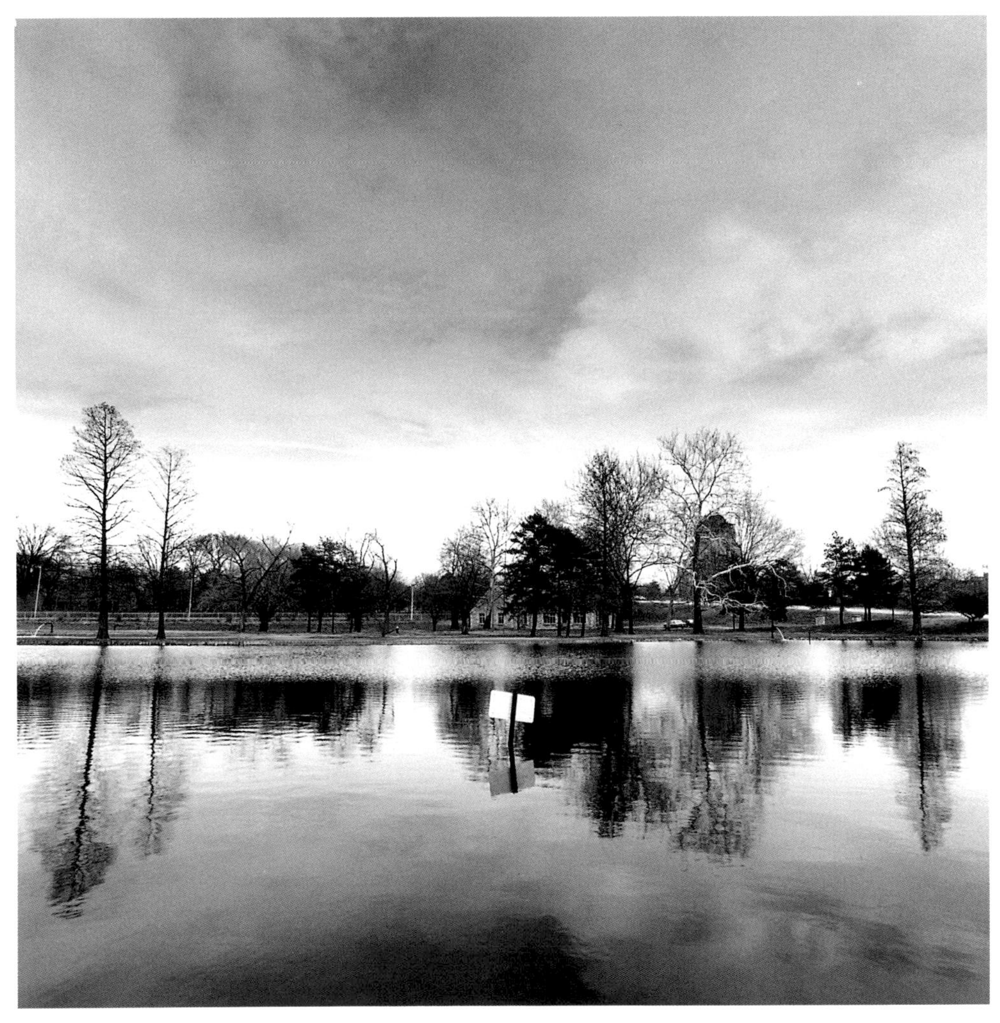

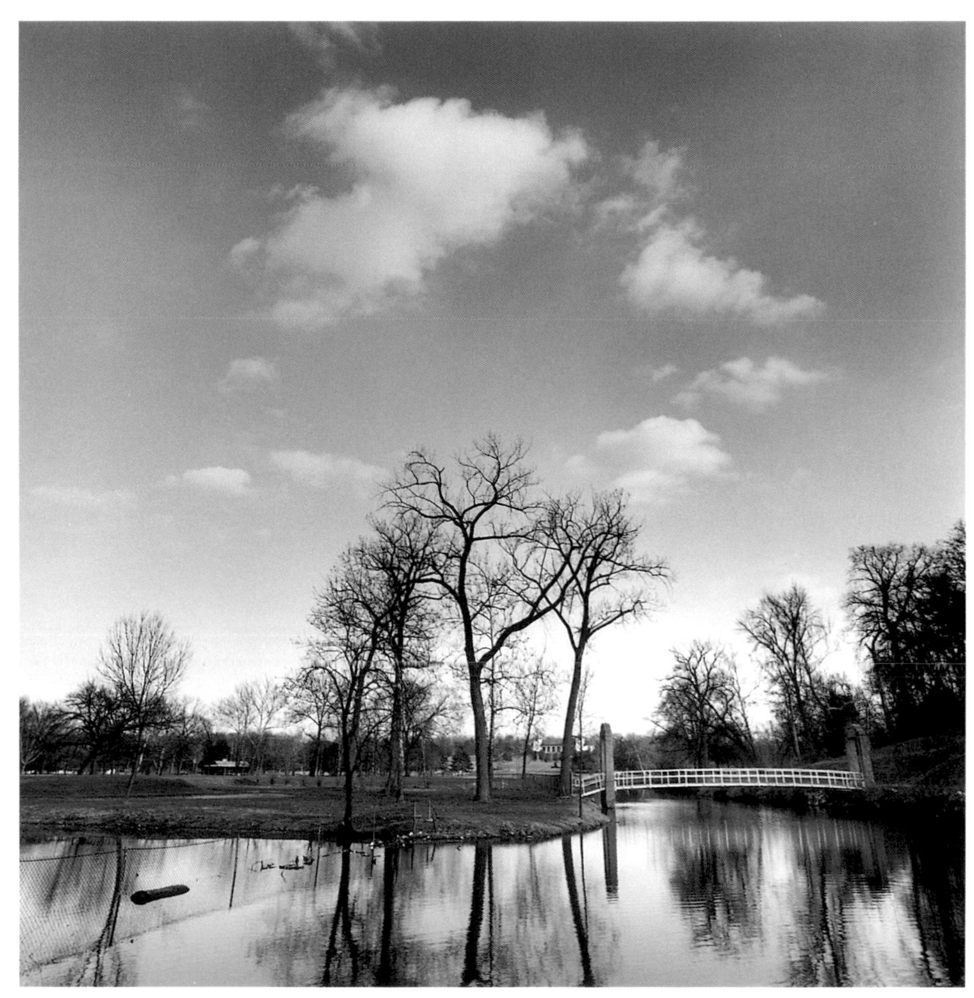

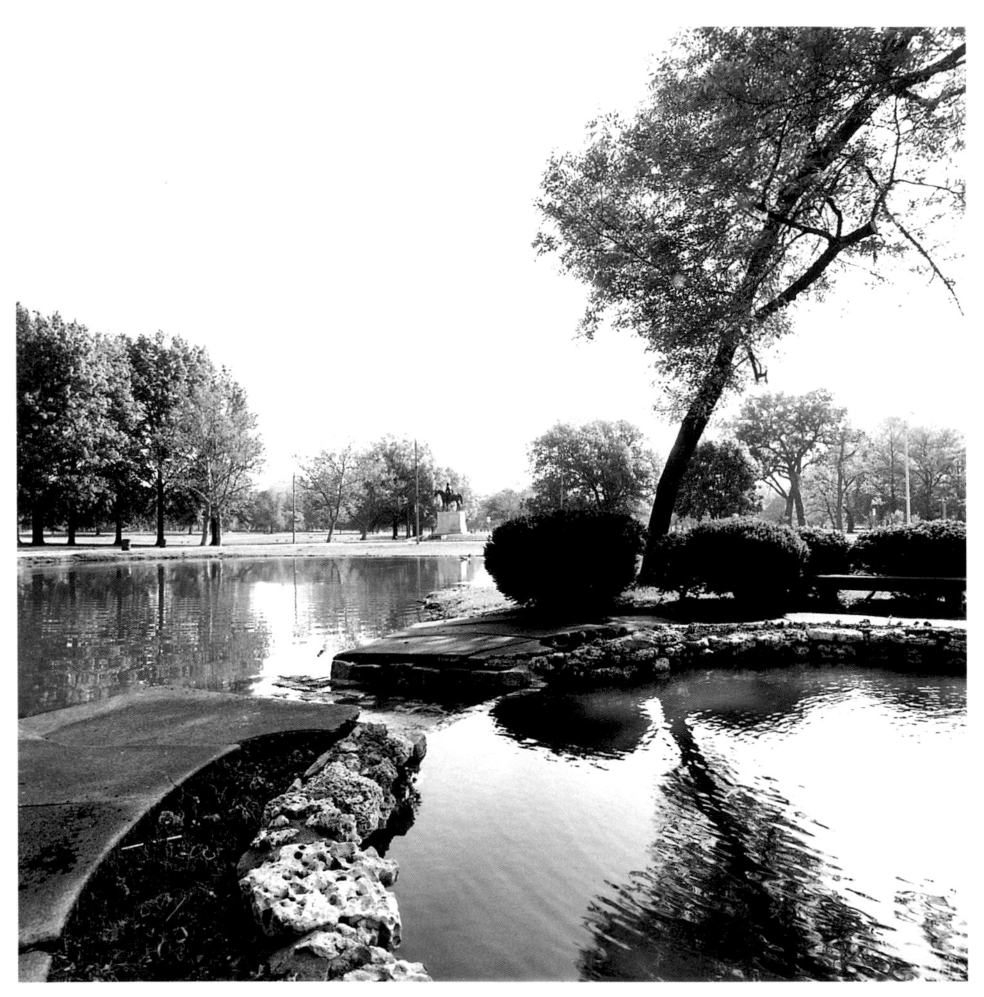

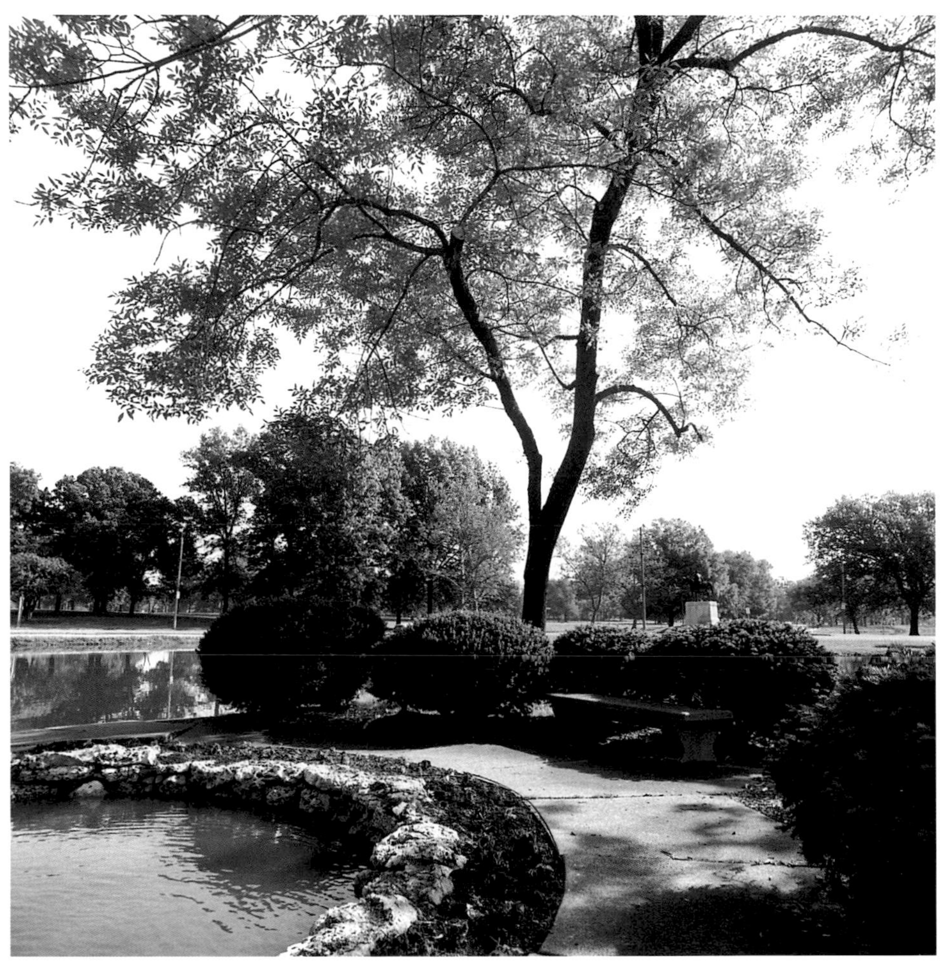

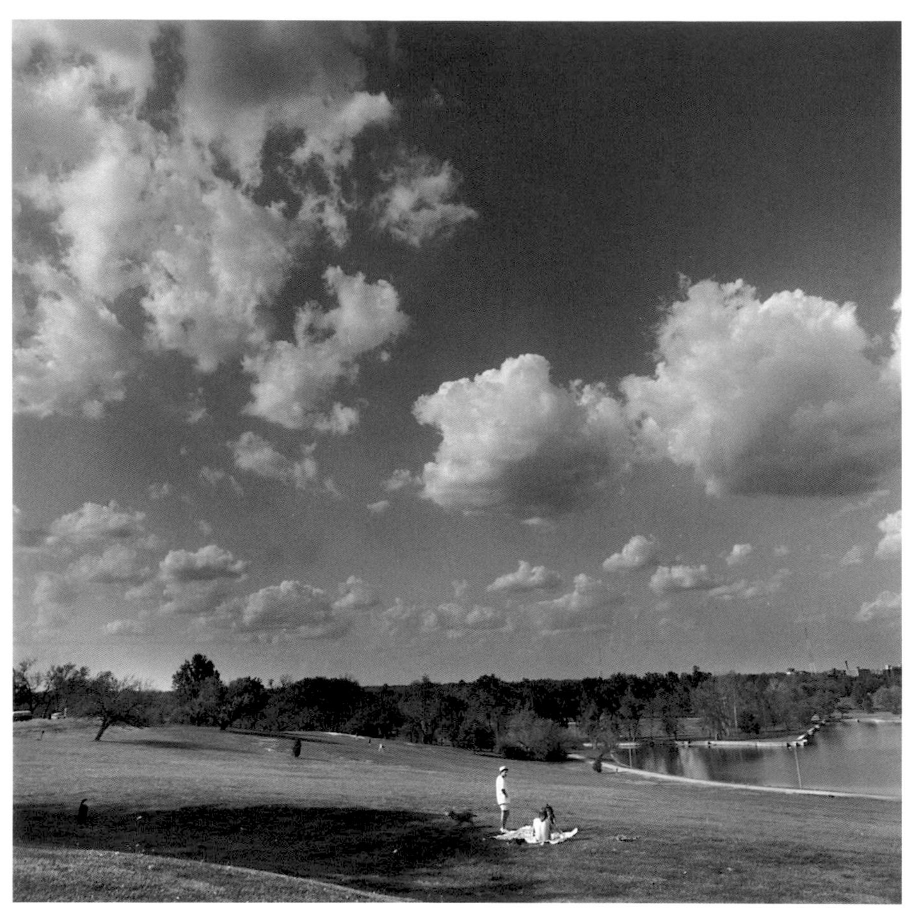

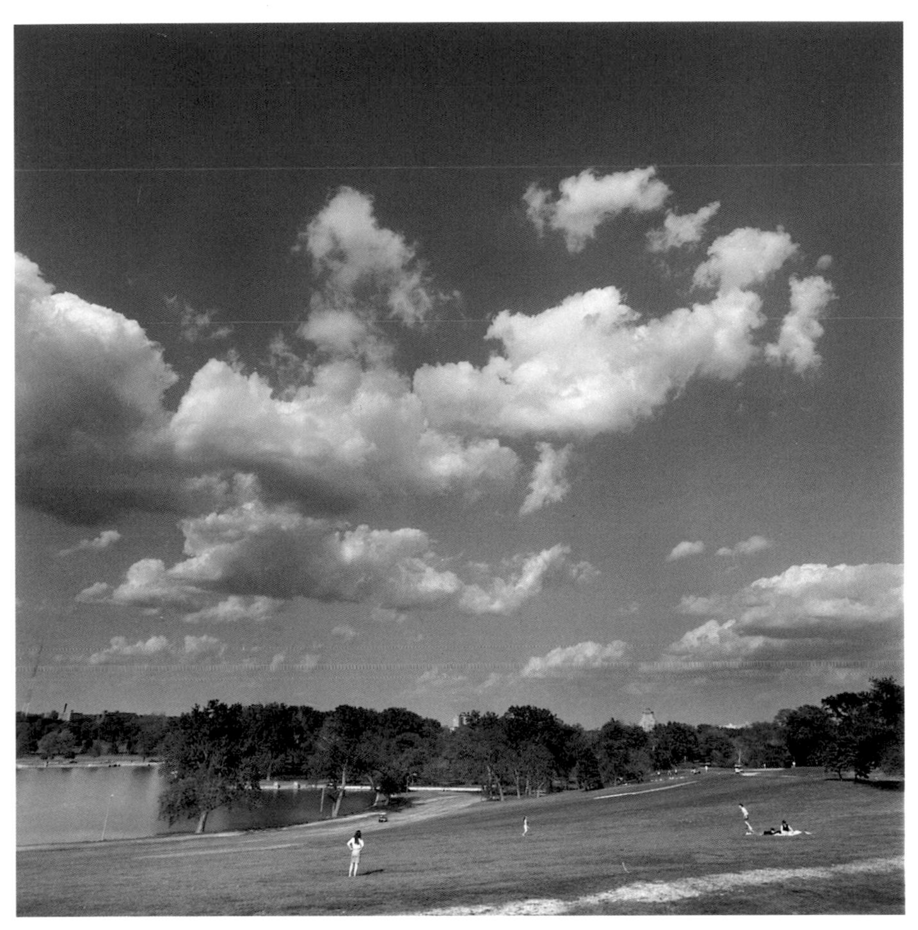

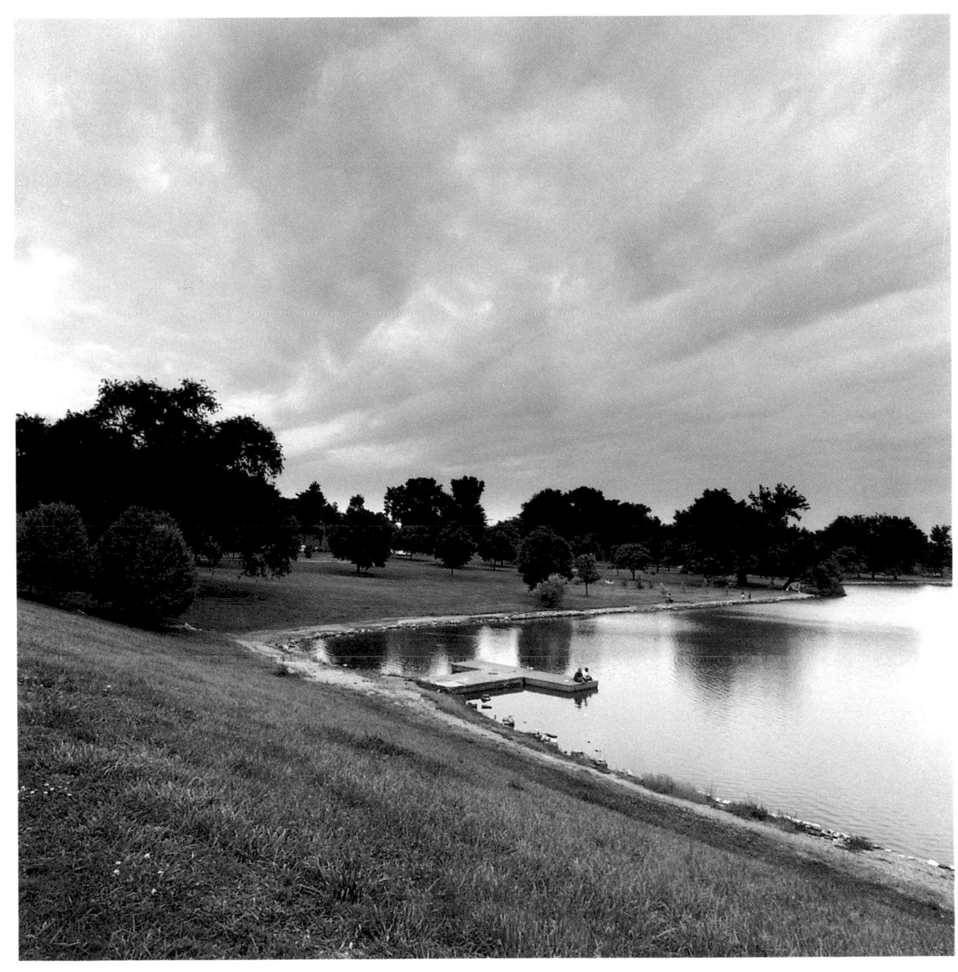

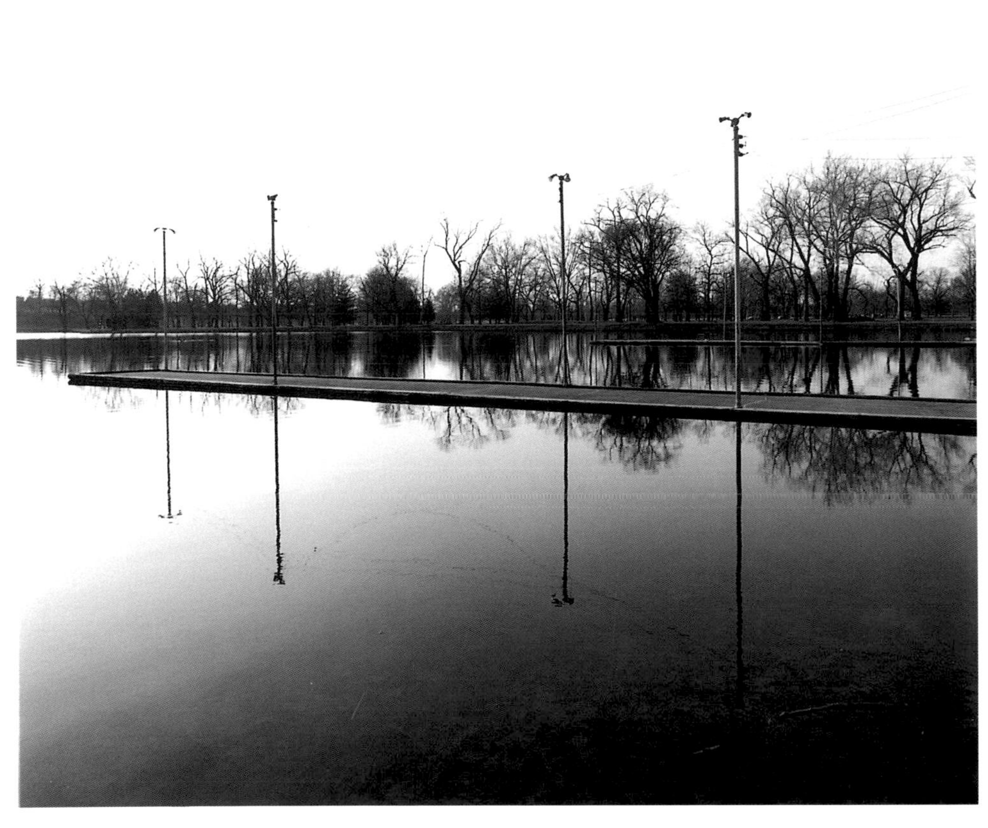

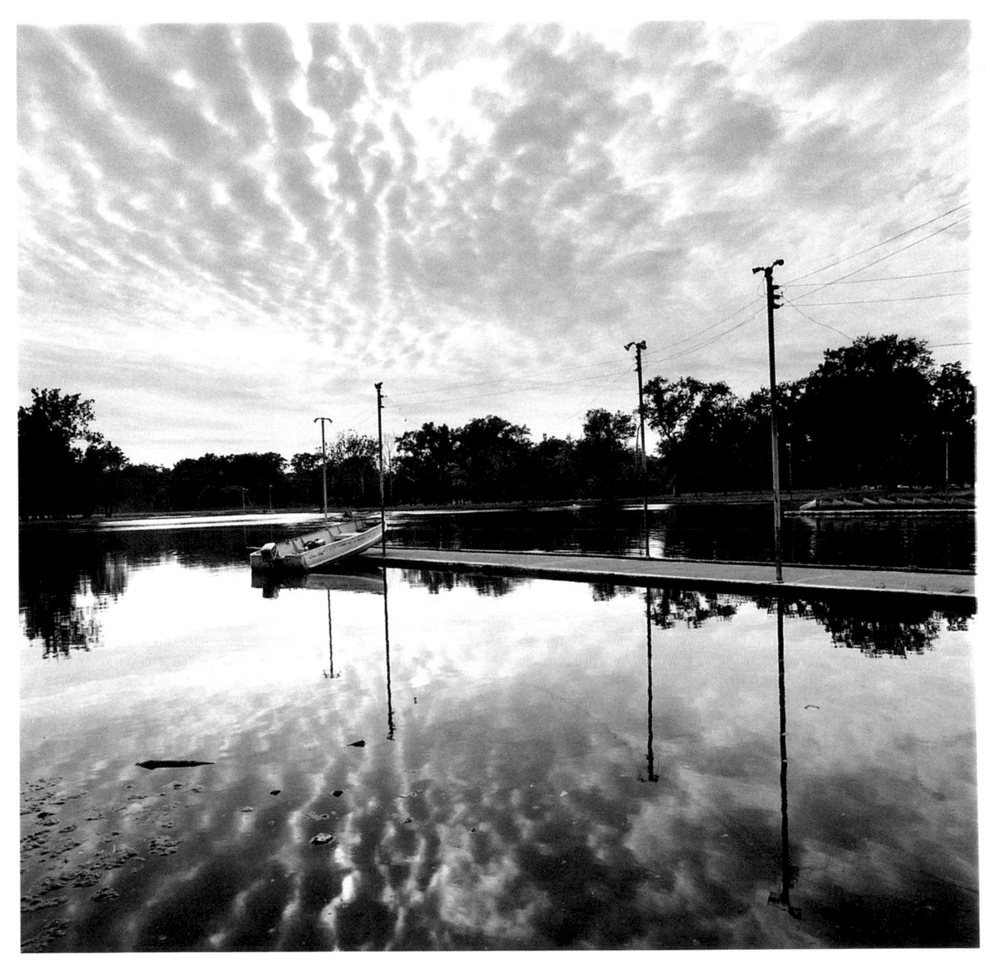

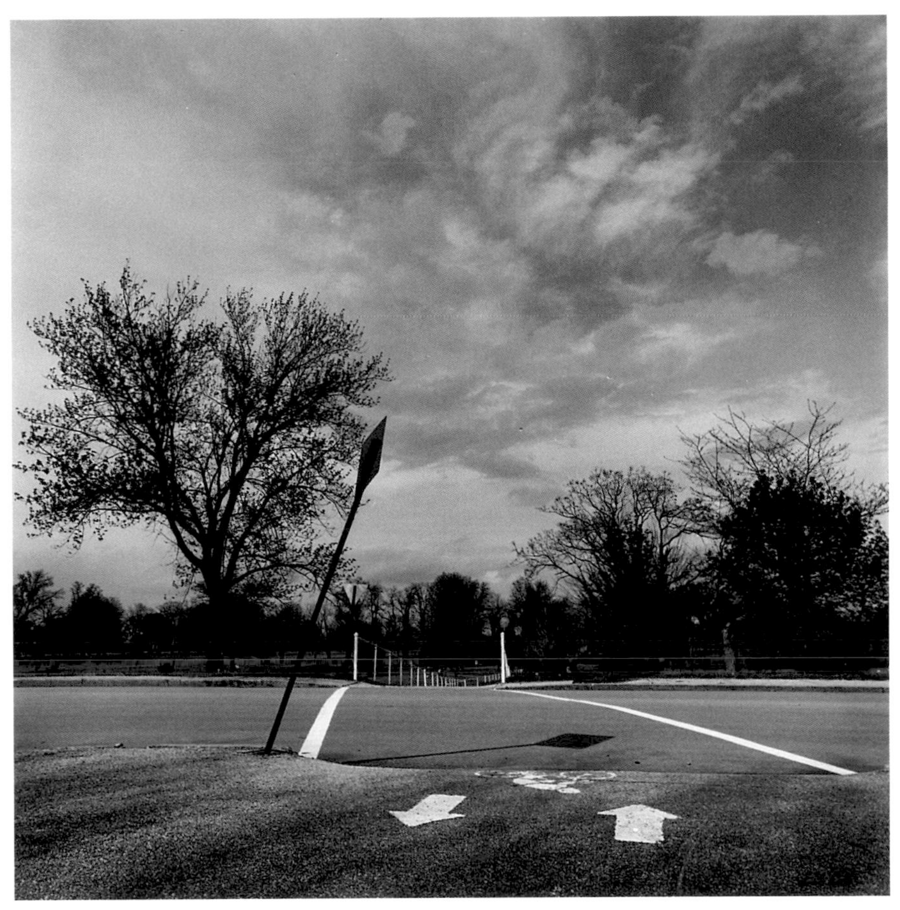

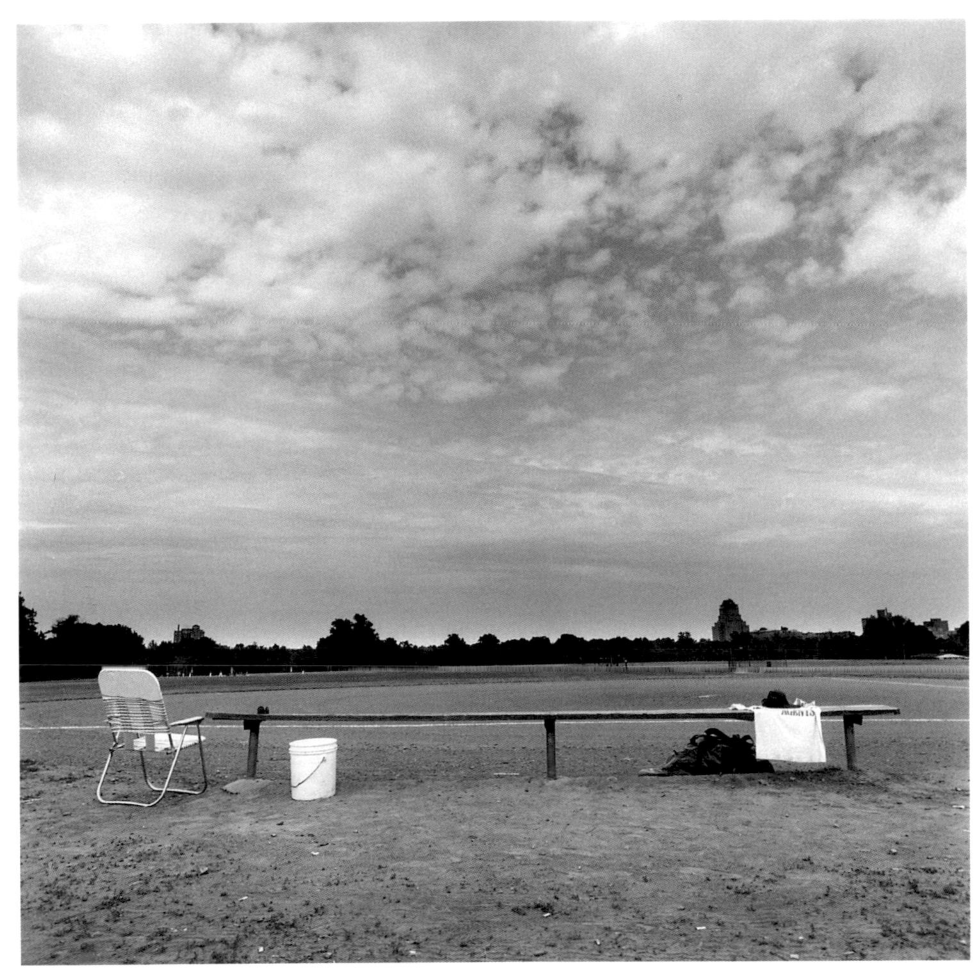

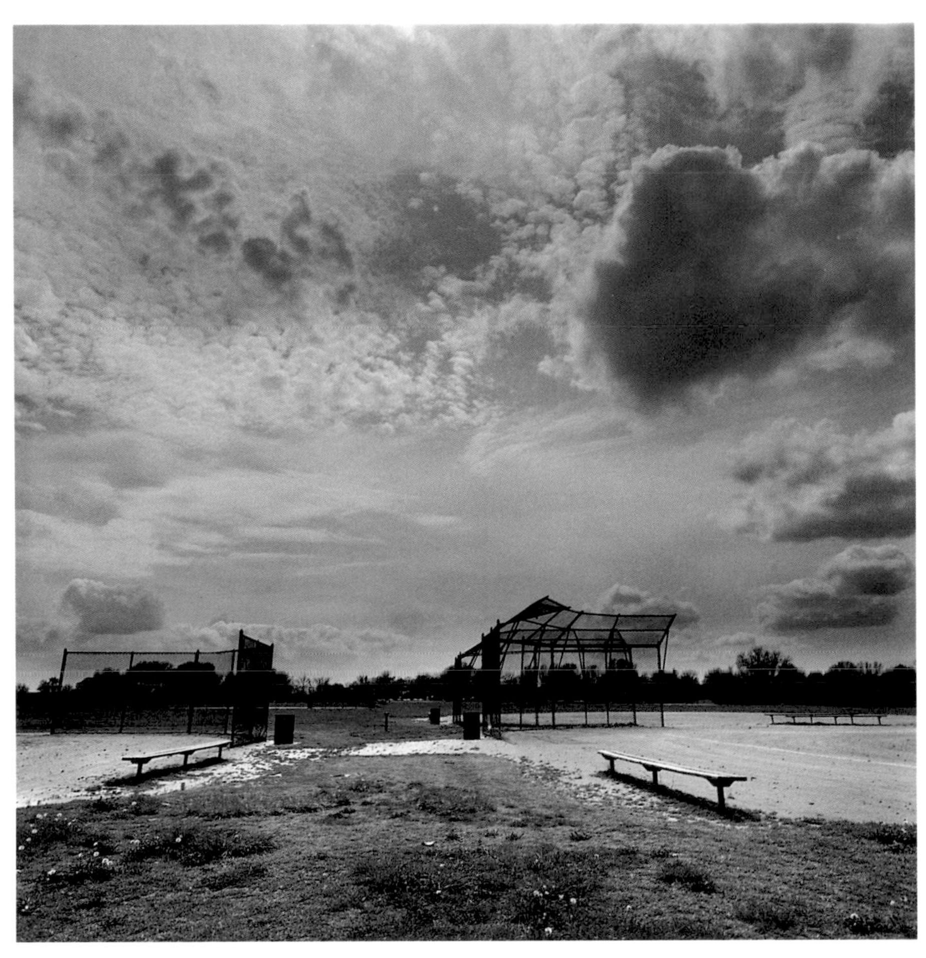

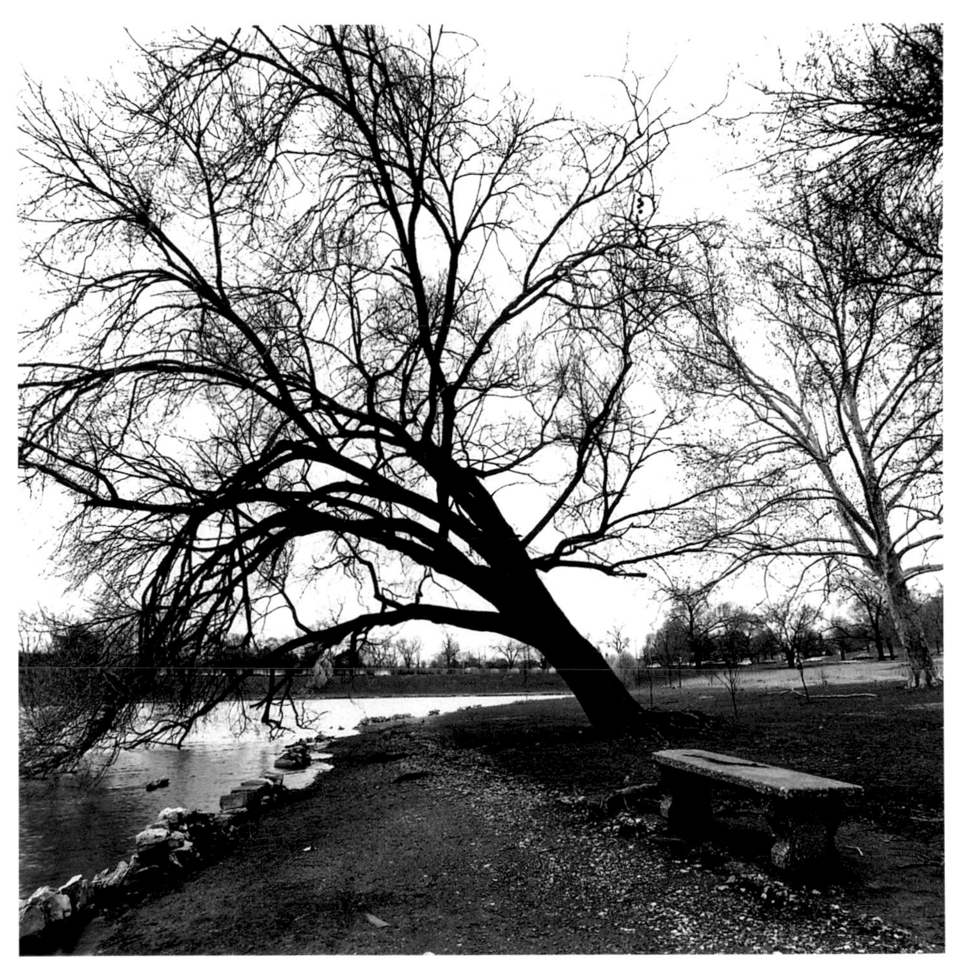

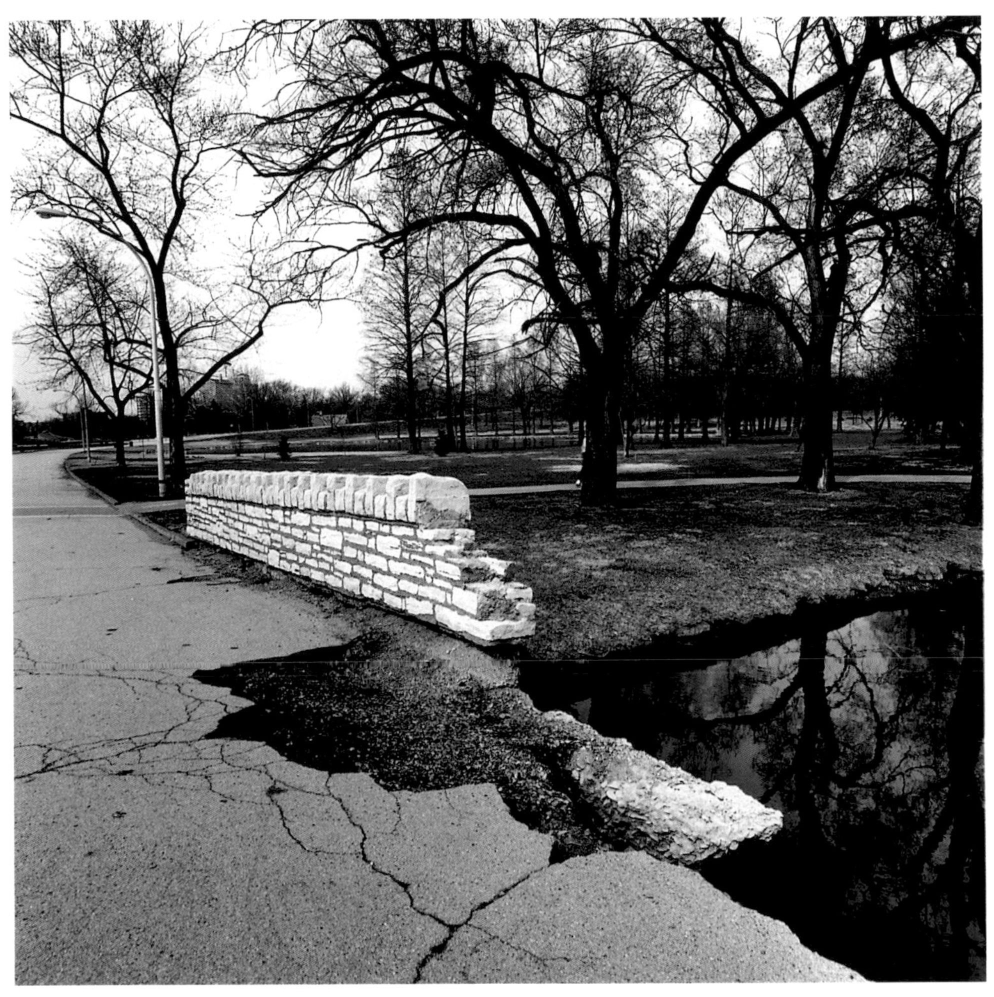

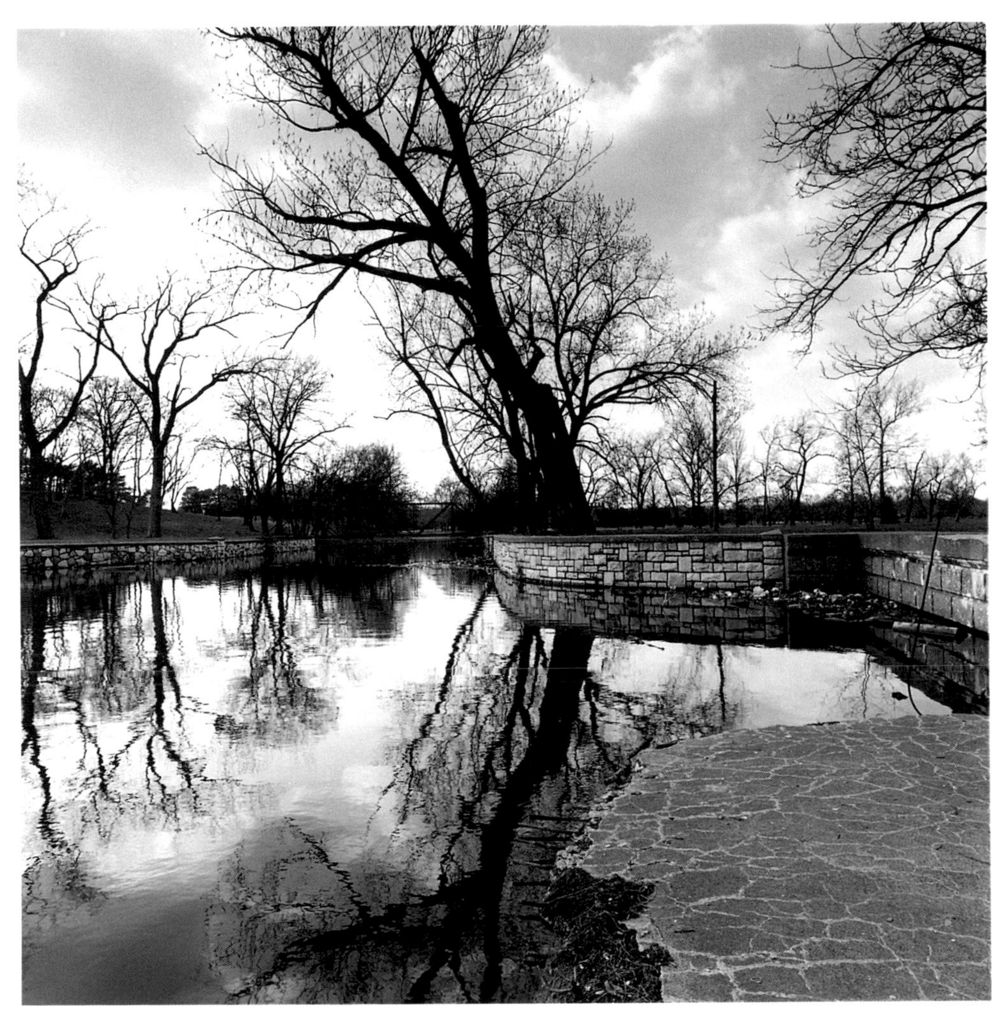

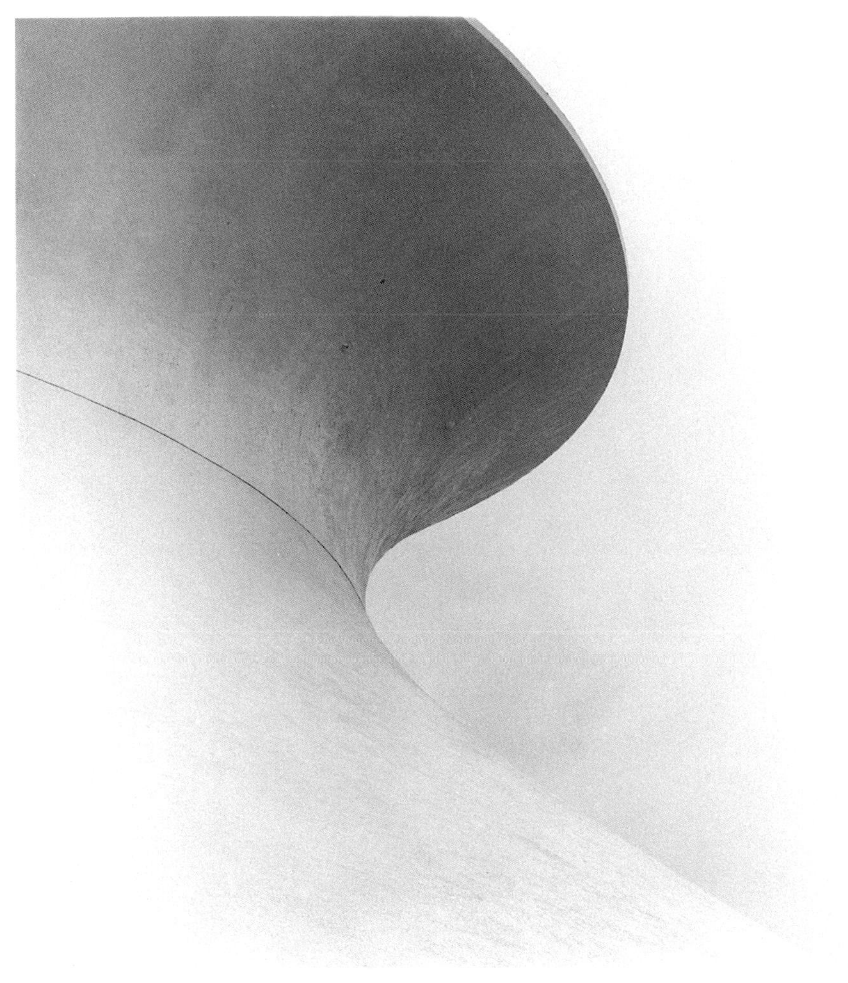

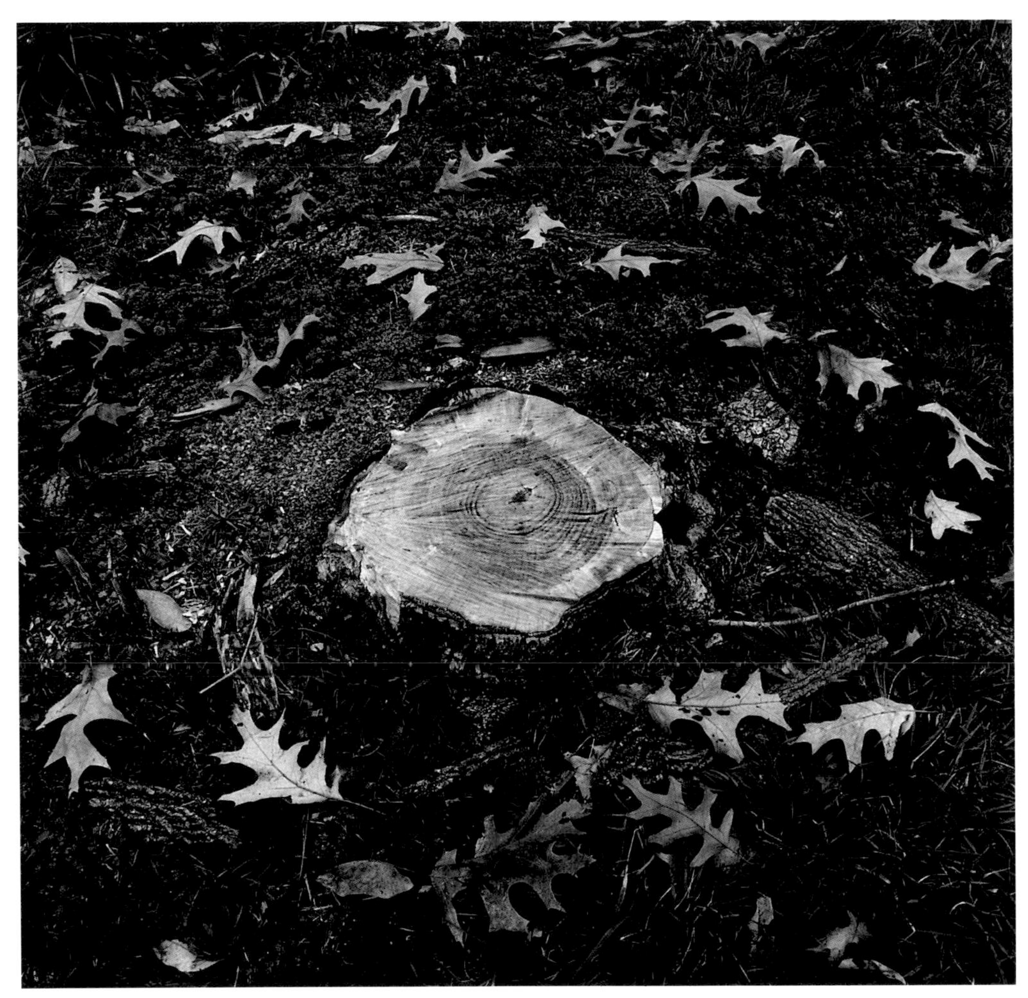

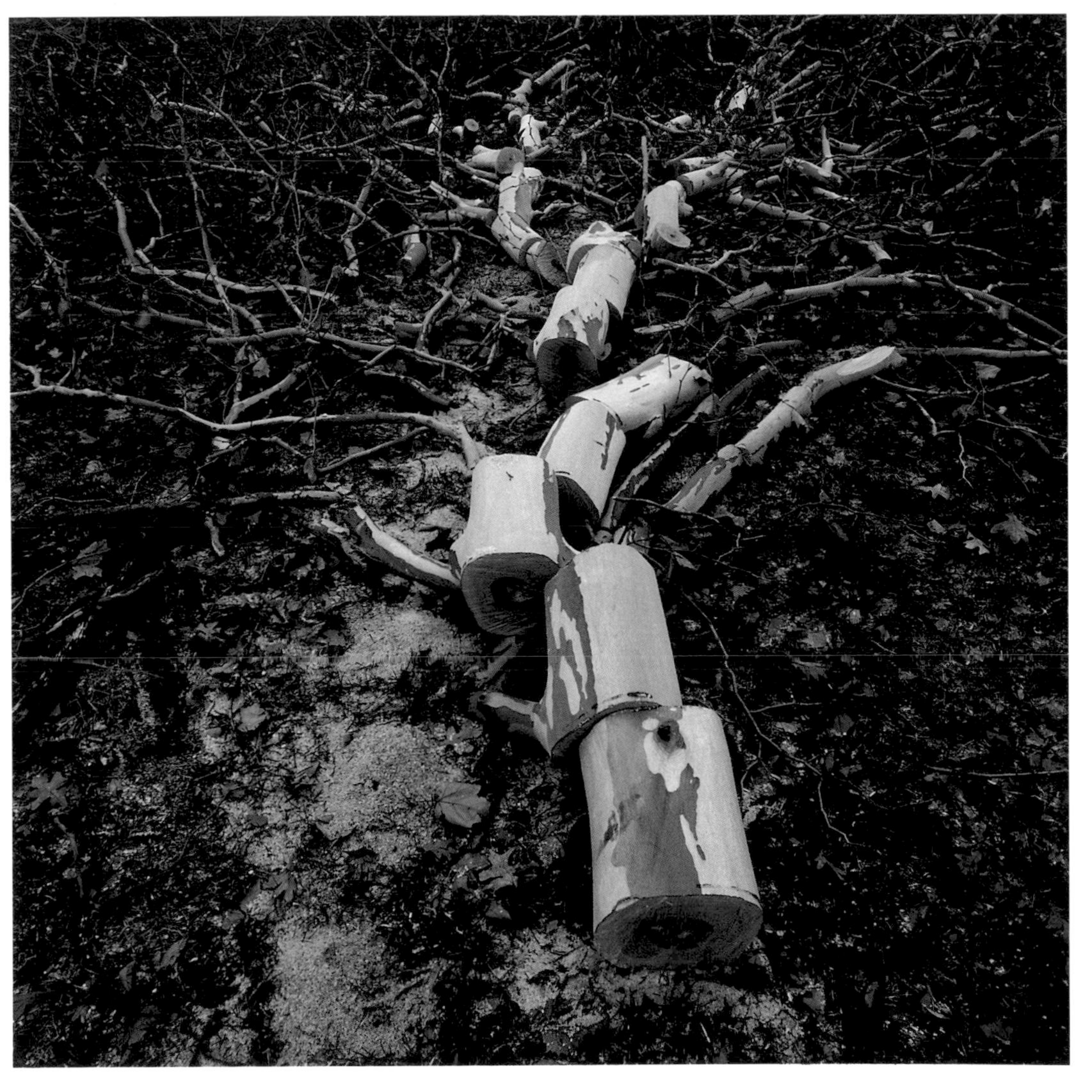

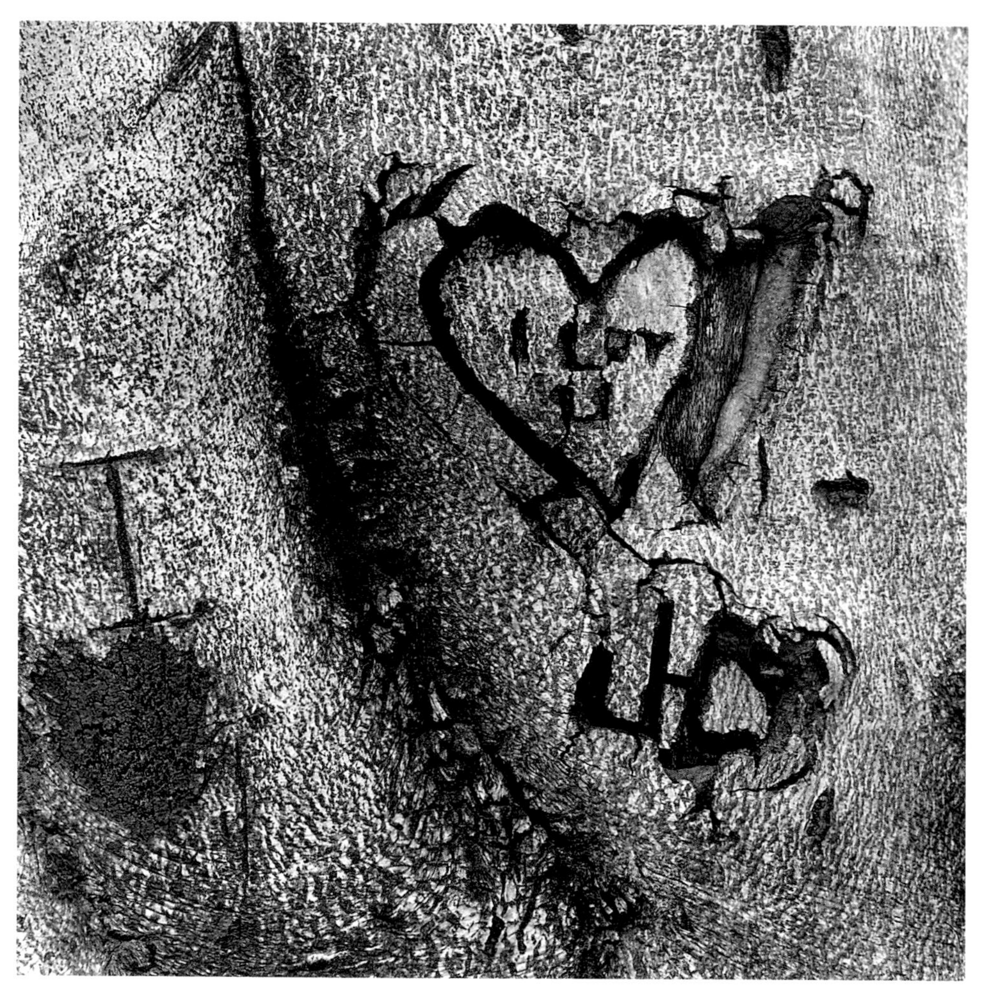

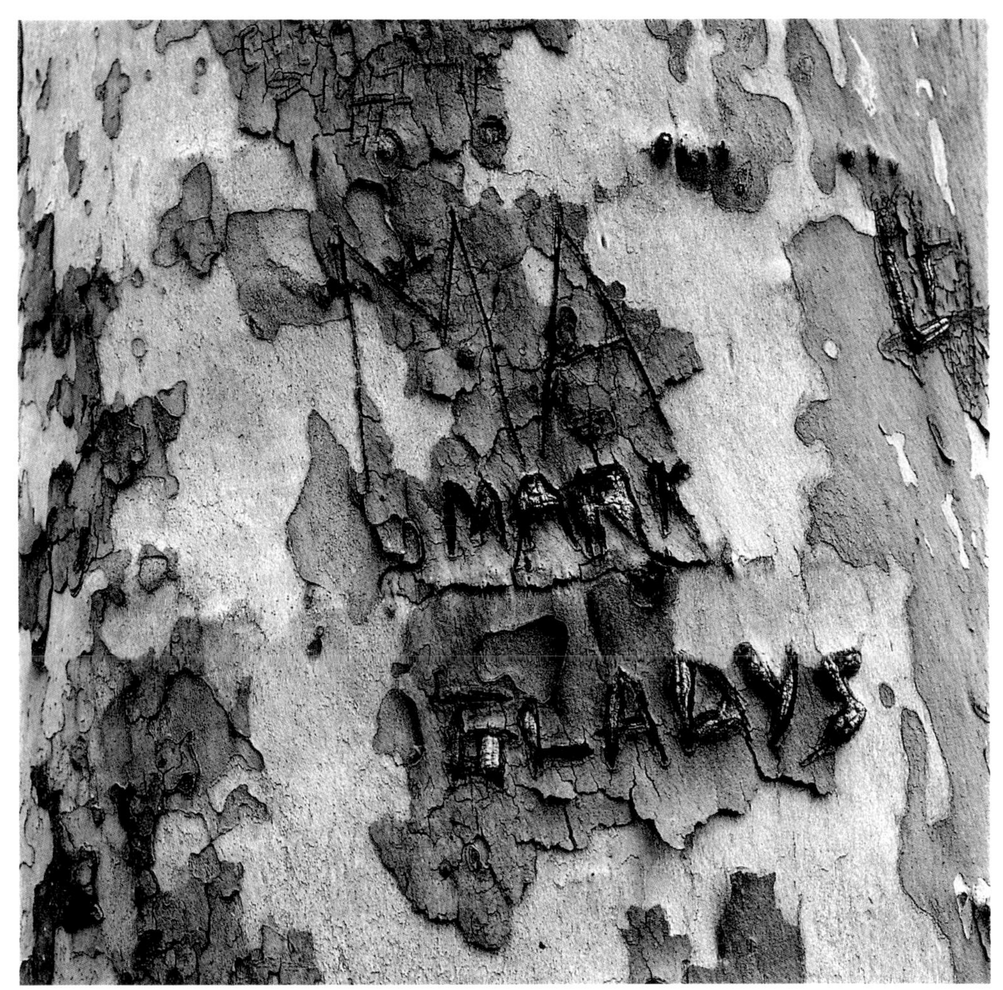
MARK
GLADYS

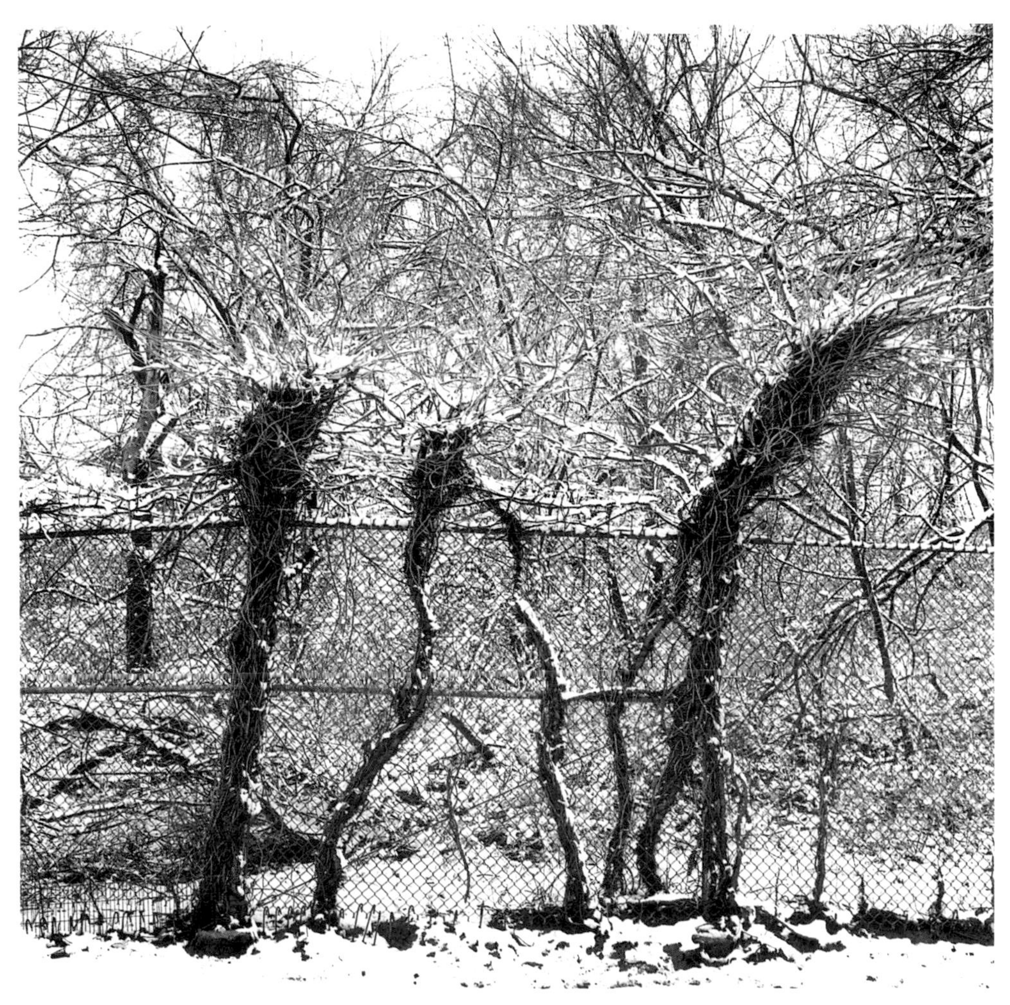

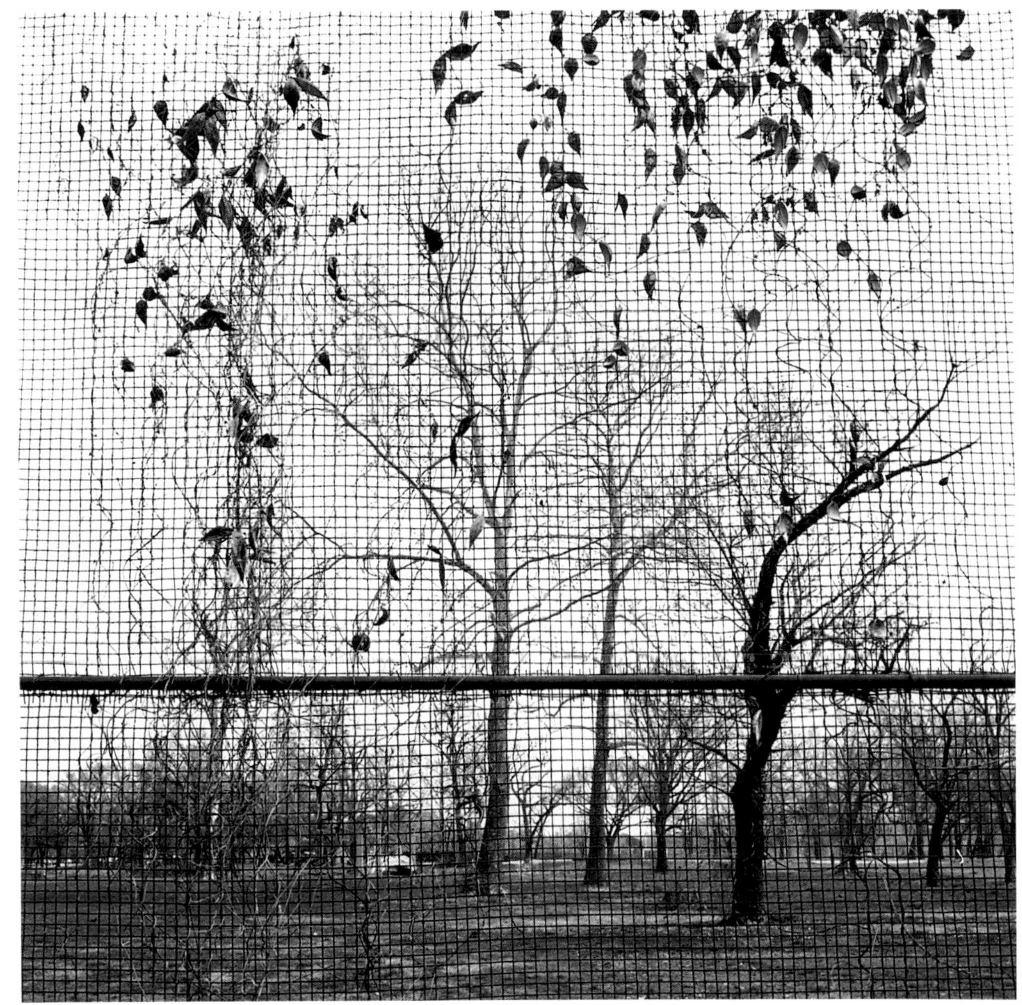

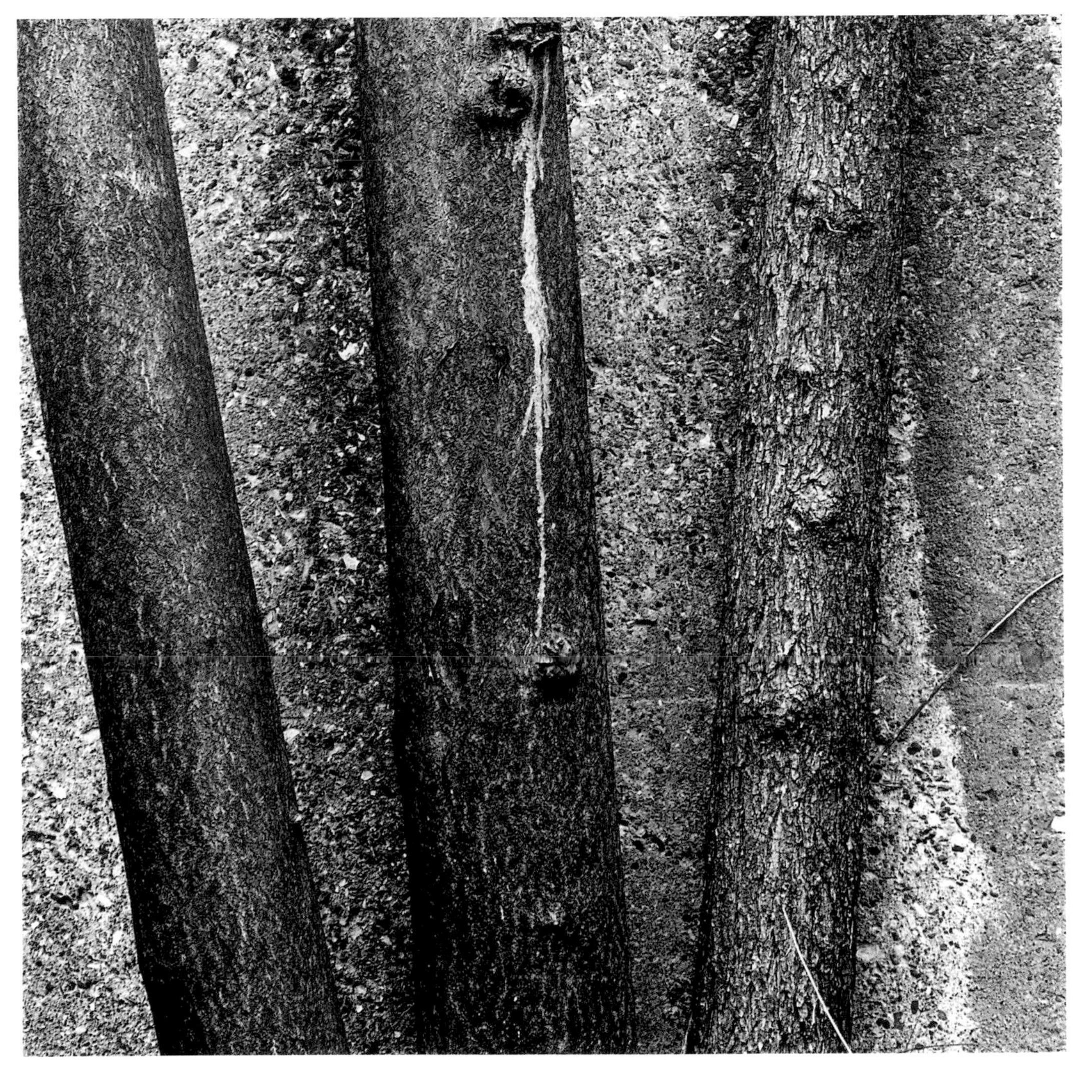

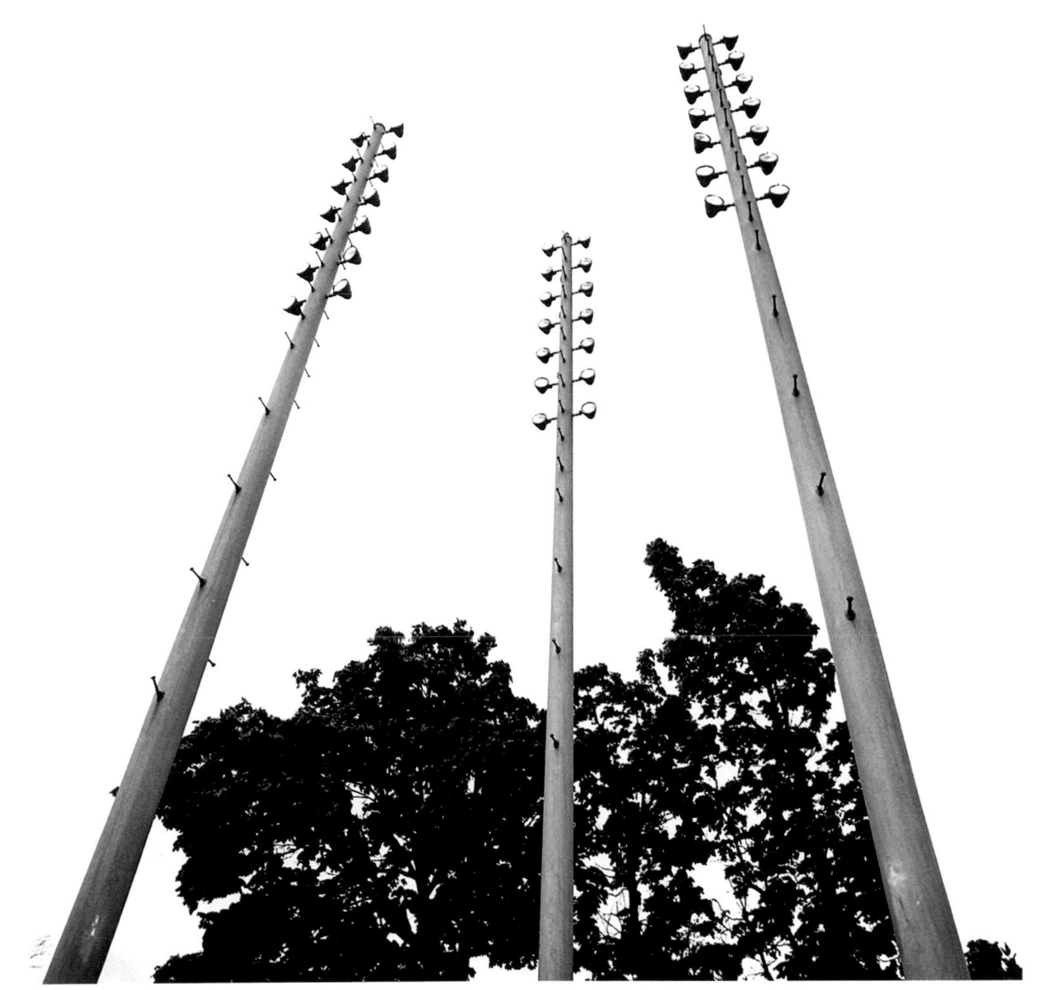

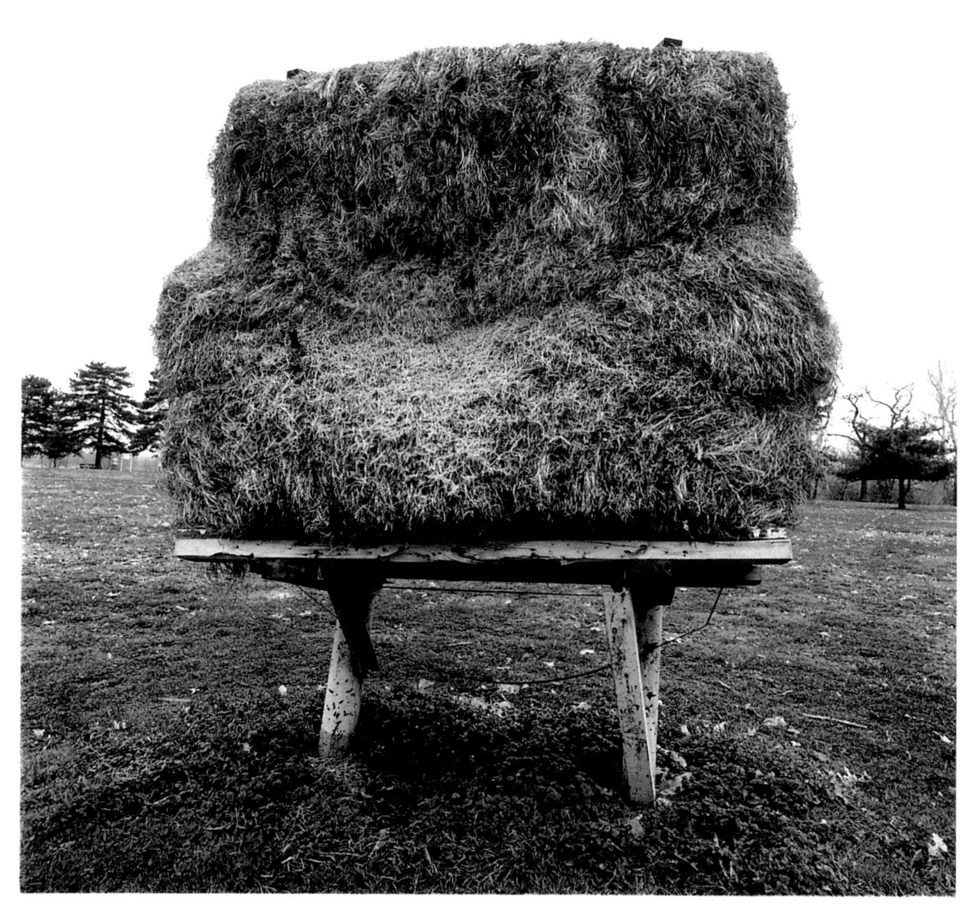

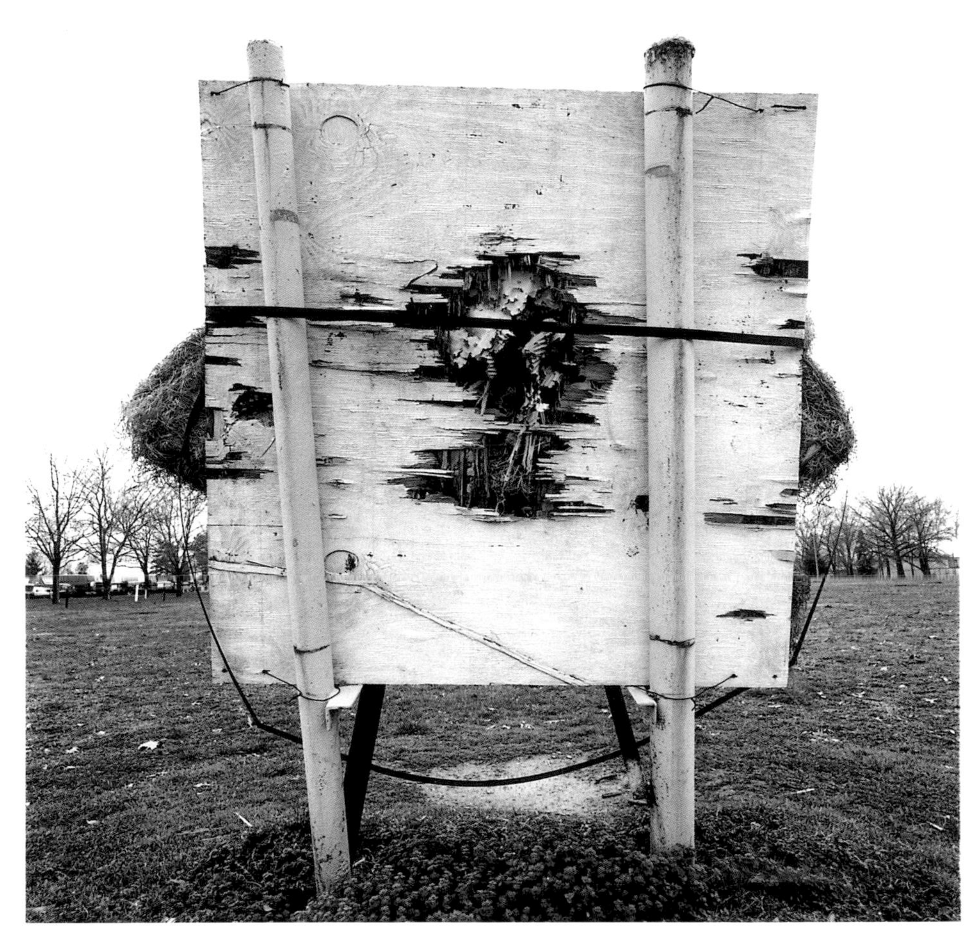

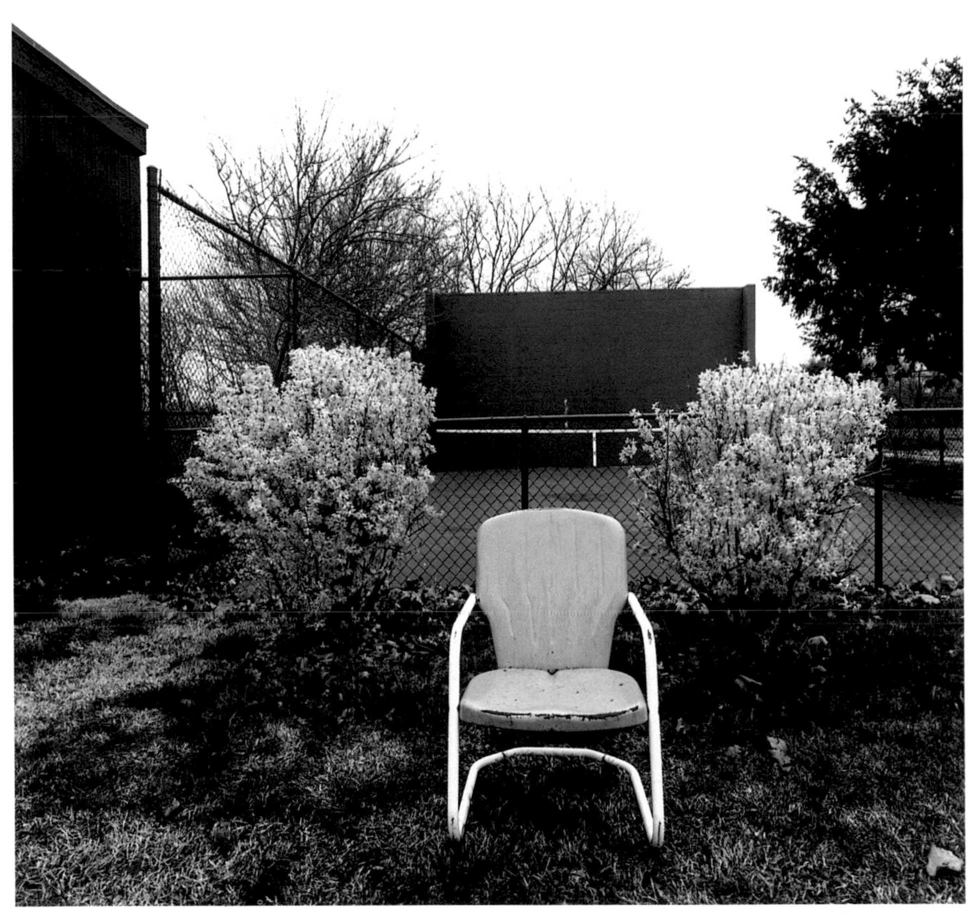

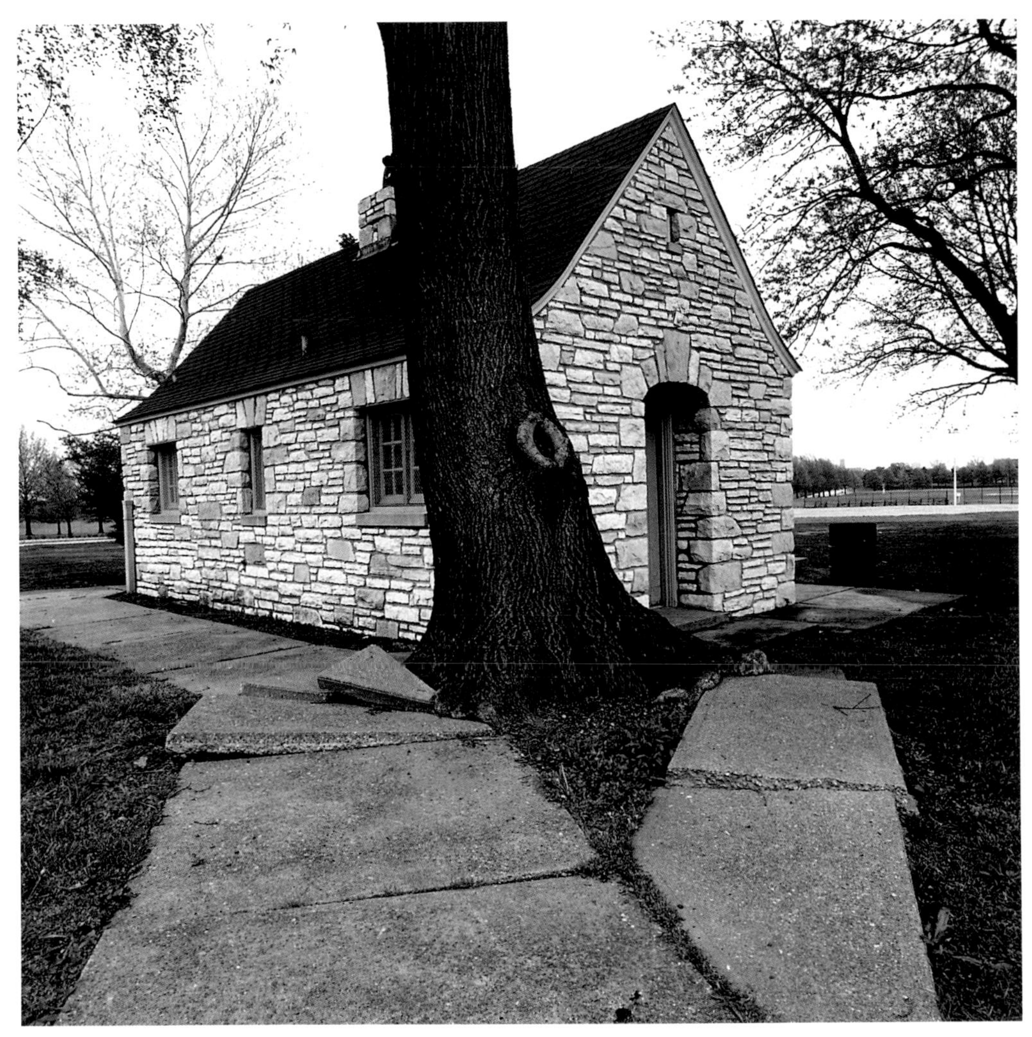

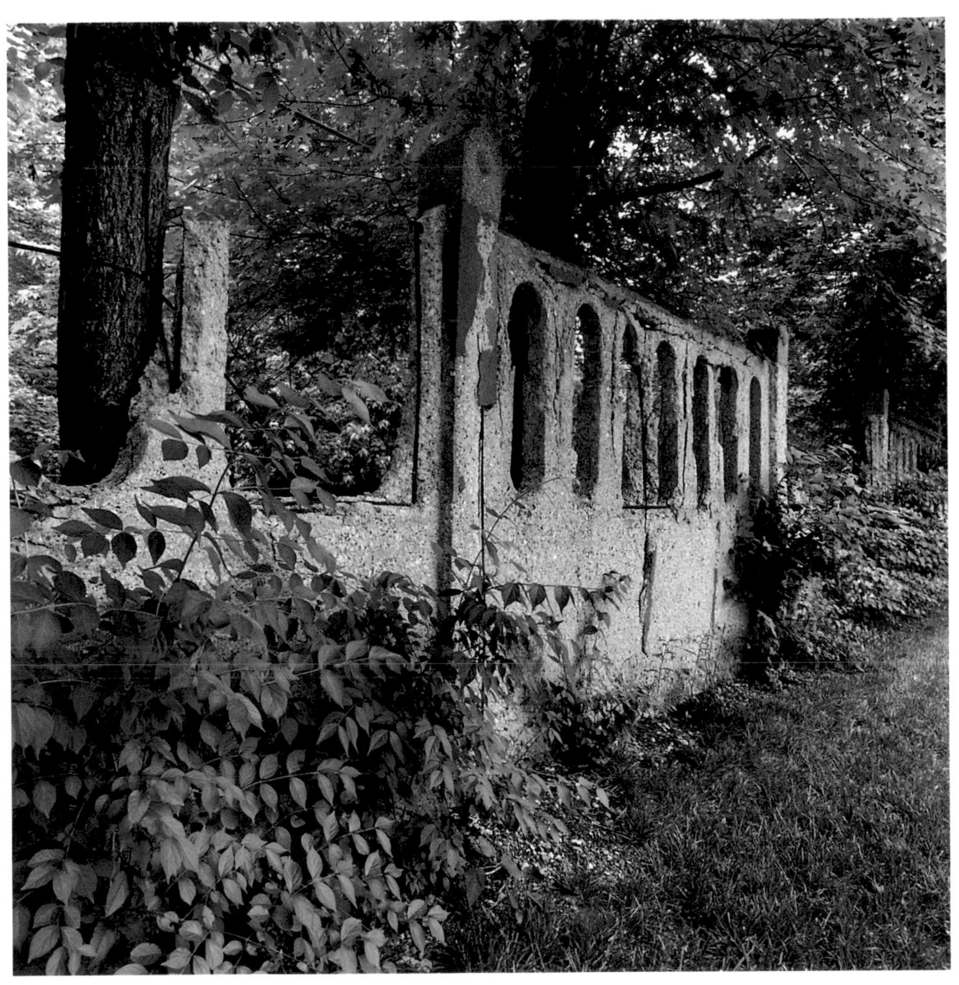